THE LAMA KNOWS
A Tibetan Legend is Born

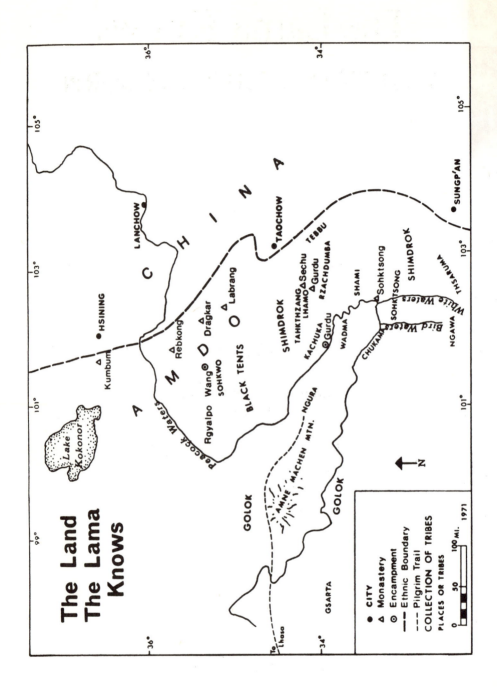

The Land
The Lama
Knows

- CITY
△ Monastery
⊙ Encampment
--- Ethnic Boundary
--- Pilgrim Trail
COLLECTION OF TRIBES
PLACES OR TRIBES

0   50   100 MI.   1971

The Lama Knows

A TIBETAN LEGEND IS BORN

ROBERT B. EKVALL

Foreword to 1981 Edition
by L. L. Langness

Chandler & Sharp Publishers, Inc.

Novato, California

To your memory, Lorraine, is dedicated
this tale of Tibet: you who first said, "That
is worth the writing" and put a pencil
in my hand.

Library of Congress Cataloging in Publication Data

Ekvall, Robert B., 1898.
  The Lama Knows.

  I. Title.
PS3509.K8L3 1981   813'.54   81-4160
ISBN 0-88316-541-4   AACR2

First Chandler & Sharp edition published in 1981.
Printed in the United States of America.
ISBN: 0-88316-541-4
Library of Congress Catalog Card Number: 81-4160

Published originally (1979) by Gulab Primlani, Oxford & IBH Publishing
    Company, 66 Janpath, New Delhi 110001, and printed at Oxonian
    Press Pvt., Faridabad, India.

FOREWORD TO 1981 EDITION

In this fascinating book Robert Ekvall has managed that which has been typically unmanageable. He has given us not only a suspenseful, unusual, and well-crafted story, but also, without didactism, an insightful view of another culture. Not a comprehensive or detailed view, of course, but what a view it is! Set in mysterious Tibet, where the author lived with the Tibetans for many years, written in a style that conveys even the nuances of Tibetan thought, Ekvall skillfully moves us along the twilight zone separating phenomenal existence and the world of illusion and belief. We are allowed to see a Tibetan legend in the making and understand the process of legend-making in the context of Tibetan views of time, space, and causation. But it is far more than a book on folklore or the tale of a Tibetan folk hero! The discerning reader will comprehend much about Tibetan social organization, politics, and religion, as well as about the intimate relationships between those institutions.

To write intelligently for a Western audience about a non-Western culture is difficult at best. To combine ethnographic fact with a compelling tale and an appropriate style, and at the same time achieve verisimilitude, is virtually impossible. To accomplish this with the parsimony and precision of a fine artist and simultaneously convey so much of universal human nature and culture must command our utmost respect. Only an anthropologically astute scholar with an intimate knowledge of the language and culture of those he writes about, and also an unusual ability to create prose, could have produced such a book. I, for one, express my admiration here and now.

The Lama Knows should take its place alongside such works as Elenore S. Bowen's *Return to Laughter* and Kenneth E. Read's *The High Valley* as one of those anthropological classics that perennially encourage that interest in other ways of life that is the soul of anthropology. Beyond that, it will afford much pleasure to anyone who appreciates a good story well told.

L. L. Langness   *March, 1981*
University of California, Los Angeles

ACKNOWLEDGMENT

No one can ever acknowledge, to the full, the debts owed to experience and persons whenever a creative effort results in a record such as "The Lama Knows," yet some attempt must be made to tot-up that indebtedness. In addition to sources that are cited, herewith my acknowledgment of what—in the making of this book—I do owe: to a haunting identification with, and longing for, the scenes and people of the land; to immersion so deep in Tibetan living that the reactions described were tested in Tibetan-style characterizations—as one rings a coin to test its genuineness —and speeches remembered, or attributed, were formed phrase by phrase in Tibetan before they were translated into English and so recorded; to a year's intensive reading of the French—Flaubert in particular—that guided me toward a narrative technique of scenes in the historical present with flashbacks to link developments in a time continuum; to Lobsang Tenzing, Tibetan artist, who listened without comment to description of scenes and, unhampered by further guidance, lined in black and white, Tibetan style, the interpretation; to the Thomas Burke Memorial Washington State Museum for permission to use some of those sketches which—for exhibition purposes—had become museum property; and to the patience and skill of Gene Turner who mapped the land—terrestrial—the lama knows. To each and all—experience and person— my corresponding gratitude.

R.B.E.

PROLOGUE

The tale here presented could come into being only in Tibet; by rumor, scornful laughter, astonishment and awe, only in Tibet could it grow into a legend; and the events on which it is based could take place nowhere else but in that far land. Thus only against the background of Tibetan culture—the way the Tibetans see the world and pattern their behavior—does it have meaning. To introduce the story properly to all who are not Tibetan, something, therefore, must be said to explain those aspects of Tibetan culture that relate to the events and the tale of "The Lama Knows," and some indication must be given of the sources on which the narrative is based.

All those who live on that high plateau which is the land of Tibet, but especially the dwellers in the black tents, know full well the realities of their life—lived at the highest altitudes and in a land of austere beauty yet battered by furious storms of wind, rain, hail, snow and dust—more often gravel than dust. With severe realism—hardy yet cheerful—they survive, and there is nothing visionary in their matter-of-fact response to the rigors of their existence, yet their conceptualization of existence is strangely beyond the facts of everyday living.

Existence is believed to be on three planes; the absolute, the relative and the imaginary. The absolute pertains only to existence in the "Buddha Field," which is the realm of final realization, or liberation, either to the ever-renewed compassion for all living beings of bodhisattvahood, or to the quiescence of Nirvana. The relative is the plane of phenomenal existence—ever uncertain yet ever moving toward the absolute. It comprehends all that can be known in the here-and-now by the testimony of the senses. The imaginary, on the other hand, is the world of illusion—all the magical manifestations that intrude into the realm of the senses. The illusions originate: in the trickery of the gods, in the psychic powers of those who have achieved control of the noumenal to make it supersede the phenomenal, and in fantasies wherein imagination wars with the real and creates its own substitutes for fact.

In the Tibetan world view all three of these planes or modes of existence have validity. Nor are the three sharply divided and fixed. The lines between them are blurred and occurrences have a strange mobility, shifting from plane to plane either to intrude upon the senses or to evade them.

A further characteristic of the Tibetan world view is the manner in which cause and portent have a relationship in which neither one has final primacy. They have a common terminology and are thought of as being basically one. Portents, or omens, as observable phenomena, are further qualified as "outer," and causes, mysteriously unobservable, are distinguished as "inner." Either one may produce the other or impinge upon it. Thus every phenomenon has a dual aspect, either as a cause moving unpredictably to produce effects, or as a portent appearing to signalize events.

Sharp reality is also challenged by the fact that all existence is thought to hover mysteriously over that strange vacuum formulated as the doctrine of The Void, which is not only the theme for endless hairsplitting and matchless casuistry but, as evidenced in everyday speech, is part of the thought world of all Tibetans. Indeed, to a surprising degree theories of existence, which in all their complexity are part of the endless debate concerning the real and the ideal, and would seem to belong only to philosophers and metaphysicians, are diffused—somewhat vaguely it is true—throughout all levels of society.

In the Tibetan world view, time too has a special quality in which past, present and future are sometimes merged, or imposed one on the other like blurred double exposures. Time is not necessarily a clear continuum along which events always follow in proper order but is modal in quality; filled with recurrences and relationships which are outside the western sense of time. "We two, father-son, ten thousand years ago were****now are****ten thousand years from now will be****" is a continuing refrain—the leitmotif—of one of the great Tibetan stories of recurrent existence unfettered by time. The sense of such persisting relationships and repetitive existences telescopes past and future into one all-embracing present.

Within that vast present of the Tibetan world view, Lama-hood, as concept and institution, is of prime importance. The term lama has been applied indiscriminately to all members of the clergy but, strictly speaking, it belongs only to the "Emanation-body" ones who, following Chinese usage, are often miscalled "Living Buddhas" and make up approximately one percent of the clergy. Lamas are not monks, although they usually observe the rules of the monastic order. They are what they are not by reason of any vow taken or slow progress made in sanctity or learning but by reason of birth; from the Dalai Lama, as the highest, to the relatively most obscure lama in some little monastery, they are all the constantly renewed manifestations of saviorhood—exemplifying the compassion of the bodhisattvas toward all living creatures.

In the sense that they are bodies they are incarnations of spirits which have achieved liberation from recurrent birth, suffering, death and the pains of hell—the dreary round of Karma-set changes on the wheel of life—and thus are free to merge into Nirvana. Yet because of their compassion for all living beings they elect to return in birth after birth as saviors so that they may aid all sentient beings in the vanquishing of ignorance and progress along the road to the same final liberation.

The "emanation-body" lamas take part in much of ritual, yet their principal role is not to administer ritual in worship—as when the monks verbalize the Scriptures for the benefit of all—but to be the recipients of worship and the dispensers of benediction and aid to all who travel the long road to final liberation. They represent the Buddhahood in living form and each one of them, in a sense and to a varying degree, by his presence in the monastery adds Buddhahood to the ever-present Congregation and Law; and thus completes the local version of the so-called Jewel Triad—more aptly termed in Tibetan "Rare-Perfect Three."

While living they are objects of worship and their position is for life. Although most of them fulfill the vows of the monastic order, they are yet above the law. An "emanation-body" lama may renounce the vows, he may break the rules, yet he is still a lama. Nothing he can do will ever make him anything less than a lama, though a monk would be unfrocked for commission of a fraction of what he may do. His reputation may suffer and his managers and tutors may deeply regret their inability to keep him within bounds, yet, even as a robber chief with many wives, he is still a lama. Many indeed may worship him with special delight and secret admiration for the power of his lamahood which makes it possible for him to muster such an array of illusions to mask the reality of his existence on the timeless plane of the absolute.

When dead—"honorably gone into the zenith"—there is no uncertainty as to what progress the lama made on the wheel of existence, for he has already achieved realization and there remains only a hushed expectation and awaiting of his return. When that return, in the body of a boy of the appropriate age, has been signalized by the right combination of prophecies, omens and personal characteristics of the newly found, he is installed in the role of his lamahood within the monastery, and one more manifestation of saviorhood has been renewed for the benefit of all living creatures.

Within the monastery of his emanation, or of his choice, each lama has his own "great house" or establishment. If, as is sometimes the case, the lama exercises political power and the functions of rule, the staff of the "great house" is organized to carry on that function. In any case the head of the establishment is a manager, usually called the ombo, who has charge of official matters and policy, arranges for the training and education of the lama, and oversees all business arrangements. The Ombo is usually a close relative of the previous lama and upon his death or retirement he is replaced by a relative of the new lama. Thus, there is an overlap in the succession of lamas and ombos which provides continuity and makes for stability in all that concerns the "great house."

The relationship of the lama and his establishment with the monastery is an association of some complexity. It is in the interest of the monastery to have one or more "emanation-body" lamas—the more renowned the better—associated with it, for although the treasuries of the monastery and the lamas are separate, yet when a resident lama is famous for his sanctity or occult power and receives much in offerings he also attracts patronage to the monastery. The lama also receives an enlarged share—fivefold is the minimum and it may be as high as ninefold—of whatever largess, received in offerings, is distributed out of the monastery treasury, for he takes part in the ritual assemblies, bringing added efficacy and blessing to such gatherings by his presence. Whenever there is only one lama—or one important one—in a monastery, there is often an even closer relationship, and the monastery may come to be identified with the lama, both being called by the same name.

These are certain essentials of the Tibetan world view—which, together with the concept and institution of lamahood, relate closely to the tale and legend of "The Lama Knows;" but there are also other predispositions and patterns of behavior which had a part in the events which took place and in the growth of the legend.

Foremost among them, as part of the strange dualism of Tibetan folkways, wherein religious aspiration and the search for the things of the psyche are mixed with assertion of the ego and lawless action, is the pattern of violence. Against the backdrop of transcendental philosophy and concepts of existence there is a savage exuberance to Tibetan living in which raiding, seduction and fighting are matters of which a man may be proud. Such behavior patterns stem from, or are linked with, delight in horsemanship and love of weaponry is linked with warlike attitudes and ministers to war—private or public.

Of the many paradoxes in Tibetan culture, one, that of the coexistence of faith with skepticism and of reverence with irreverence, is of particular importance. The average Tibetan is devoutly committed to the attitude—more aptly defined in his speech as "manner-change"—of faith-reverence, and the depth of that devotion is amply attested by the magnitude of his religious observance; yet on many occasions, almost as by compulsion, his conversation fairly crackles with outrageous irreverence and impudence, and nothing seems sacred.

From the years of my life among them I recall one incident which exemplifies this trait and which is most aptly and closely linked with the institution of lamahood. I once accompanied some Tibetans as they rode to welcome a new lama who, as a boy of seven, had just been ransomed from his family and was being brought to his "great house." My particular companion was a nomad who was splendidly mounted and proportionately prideful, yet when the lama passed, in an instant, with a torrent of praying, he was off his horse and bowed to the ground in abject worship. Later, once more ahorse, I queried him about the ransom—its size and why it was paid. His answer was something far-removed from prayers and worship.

"That is just like buying a mdzo-mo (milk cow). First you

pay for her, and if she is good you pay much, and then you milk her for butter which is wealth. Now that they have paid for the lama he will be used to produce wealth. If he is good much wealth—only the lama knows how much—but it's just like the business of a milk cow. A good one gives much, a poor one gives little. Astonishing it is—the lama knows—the lama knows." His face crinkled with amusement and impudence and then he went back to his praying.

Coupled with this irrepressible irreverence which seems to characterize most Tibetans—particularly the people of the black tents, whose ways are wilder and whose tongues are more untamed—they have a keen sense of the ridiculous and a wary appreciation of how much ridicule can do to damage status and reputation.

As a last item in this list of culture traits, the special fascination which Tibetans feel for language and all its uses plays a distinctive role in the story of "The Lama Knows." At every level of Tibetan experience, speech is of great importance. The power of speech, the power of thought and the power of action—or mouth, mind and body—make up the triad of personal being. Verbalization is the first and most important of the works of religion by which virtue-merit is accumulated and progress along the middle way is assured. Oratory and powers of debate and exposition make for advancement in the religious and political hierarchies, and the word well-spoken gets universal hearing and commands deep respect. Story telling and prosody are highly developed, and the one who is truly able and influential is the one who has "mouth-face" and can make words serve him well. Commonality of language is one important aspect of the Tibetan self-image, or cultural self-identification, yet the Tibetans have vast admiration for one who speaks many languages; and some of the greatest figures in Tibetan history were known as the "interpreters." They also admire the use of dialects and different styles of speech to suit different occasions or serve different ends, as they savor to the full the supreme magic of words.

It is in this varied and distinctive cultural atmosphere that the events of the developing tale took place and gained a telling—altogether Tibetan in its sources and viewpoint—growing, as it was told, into a legend in the folklore of a people, and aptly characterized by the universal Tibetan exclamation of wonder and astonishment—"The lama knows!"

Picaresque tale, or legend in the making, the story is not, in any case, the product of imagination. It does at times appear to wander into the realm of the illusory, yet basically it is a record of phenomenal happenings, and tells of actual persons and their deeds—some real and some ascribed. Thus, it was from many sources that I put together the amazing whole of this Tibetan saga. I had first-hand access to some events and to many personages of the story. Much more was told as news, passed on as rumor, or debated with sudden unexpected intensity by those who gossiped, jested and argued, as they drank their tea in my guestroom, during the whole length of the time I lived in Tahk Thzang Lhamo and traveled among the people of the tents in northeast Tibet.

I never met that lama, who came to be called the "Earless One," face to face, yet from an inconspicuous place among the spectators I did see the ordeal of his trial. I heard too his amazing defense, in which he employed all the resources of speech and the changing magic of words. Nevertheless, long before that I had heard about him and the mystery of his appearance. At the time I explored the Drag Kar caves, all the way to the "sea of darkness," the monk-guide from the Drag Kar monastery told me about the strange figure who was found sitting in the mouth of the cave with the unbroken, untracked snow spread around that entrance. In the monastery guestroom, during the course of a long talk-filled evening I also heard—in much detail—of gifts offered to the one who had come and asked for nothing, yet willed bestowal waves of blessing like a veritable lama.

Later from traders who went on successive trips to the salt lakes of the north I heard more of "the lama who had come" and of his ways of living: of the color-matched beauty of his golden *mdzo* pack-oxen and milch cows; of the excellence of his horses; of how he rode, armed like a layman and alone, on his own mysterious concerns; of the daughter of Rgyal-wo Wang—seduced and wedded; of the wonder of his speech in three languages; and of the transcendental wisdom of his divination and forecasts which—"like successive drops of rain"—matched events that followed.

I knew full well, moreover, the consternation his appearance in the cave entrance created in Gurdu, for my house in Tahk Thzang Lhamo was within a few hundred yards of that monastery, and I was well acquainted with the steward and the ombo, and the internal intrigues of the Gurdu Great House. When they visited in my guestroom the monks of Gurdu dared not talk openly about the lama who claimed he was their lama and had returned, but when alone with me, and assured of privacy, some did talk and even jested on the brink of the unthinkable. The monks, moreover, of Sechu—a separate polity and jealous rival of Gurdu—very much enjoyed their rival's unhappy dilemma; gathering, embroidering, and passing on every bit of news and rumor—but especially delighting in ridicule. Moreover, Tahk Thzang Lhamo—a complex of two monasteries, trading posts and hamlets—was a place where many gathered from near and far, and among all who came the one who had news to tell was the most welcome.

The night the claimant lama was brought a captive—riding tied to his horse—the sound of hoofbeats had scarcely passed before the news was spread with—as part of the telling—wonder and pity as to his probable fate. The details of his torture were soon known, and there was much speculation as to how long his life would last. In the arguments which went on at times in my guestroom, even some of the fiercely partisan Tebbus took part, and voiced bloodthirsty threats about how they would use their swords to settle, once and for all—the question about the true Gurdu Lama. But even as they blustered, others—their fellow guests—taunted them with the widespread uncertainty that would not rest.

It was not only Tibetans who talked. After the Chinese general had finished humbling the Gurdu Lama and his entourage, and had lectured them on political science and the basic rights of prisoners, he stopped at my place to tell, in casual fashion, his version of what he had just done: a story I had already heard from several quite breathless Tibetans—awestruck at what had taken place and seeking my advice and intervention. Over cups of tea it was agreed—in sententious Chinese aphorisms—that the Tibetans—as all barbarians—needed enlightenment and some civilizing; at least he had done his best to begin the process. Even as he sipped his tea the ombo, his hands tied behind him, stood in the courtyard.

I knew Yzimba, aging chief of a tribe and father of lamas, quite well. I had camped at his tent door, receiving his hospitality and protection, and in much talk he told me how his son had indeed been discovered to be the Gurdu Lama and had later disappeared, but he avoided characterizing that disappearance. His other son, Ah Ta the bold—hearty and enigmatic by turns—visited me more than once and in our talk we sometimes diplomatically skirted the subject of the person, destiny and whereabouts of the Earless One, but he told me little. On the other hand many of his tribesmen would freely speculate about the future of the Lama with a disputed name to whom they felt an instinctive partisan allegiance. One of them with whom I had ridden on an all-day gazelle hunt had ridden on another day with Ah Ta to the "burning of the Buddha" and had heard of strange drunken mumblings by Musa the lighter of fires.

The Ngawa king on the other hand visited me at the time of the trial and was guardedly talkative—almost as though seeking advice. The following summer, I camped for days at his palace door and once, with little comment, he told me of the escape which failed for want of a file. About the final escape he was deadpan and noncommittal and to the question, "How did it happen?" he smiled briefly—looking me straight in the eyes and murmuring, "The lama knows." Others, even those of his court, talked more freely; wondering why the monk who helped that attempt—and mistake—had not been punished. The king's steward, still in power, adroitly avoided any discussion of the disappearance of his prisoner from his warriors' camp in the wide valley of Bird Waters, but among the warriors there were those who also wondered how they themselves had escaped being fined or reprimanded.

On the way to Ngawa that summer I visited a number of tribes—Kachuka, Chukama, Shami—and heard much talk; partisan, amused, sometimes slightly sardonic, but often increasingly credulous—as conversation unrolled like a ball of yarn from a spinner's fumbling fingers—about the mystery of the Earless One; I was even shown the spot on the banks of Peacock Waters where tracks had led through the snow to the water's edge.

I visited, too, the Sohktsong chief but we talked only of horses for I wanted one of the long-eared grays for my own use. Nanjor, his son, seemed impressed by my selection and remarked that the horse I wanted was like one once ridden by the Gurdu Lama. He refused, however, to specify which Gurdu Lama but grinned and suggested that I had heard, perhaps, of several Gurdu Lamas.

Even Musa the Moslem was an acquaintance, but about the Gurdu Lama and all his concerns—including the lighting of a certain fire—he would not talk. For one of Musa's known gifts

as a raconteur and purveyor of news that very silence had, perhaps, its own special significance.

All that I heard in rumor and spontaneous story telling, and
all that rubbed off on me, in awareness and by association, gave
me the unique experience of seeing a series of events linked, from a
purely Tibetan point of view, into an unbelievable tale; and of
sensing how a legend comes into being—and grows bit by bit—in
the folklore of a people. What is here written is an attempt to
pass on that experience. How successful the attempt is, you, the
reader, may judge, but only "the lama knows."

THE LAMA KNOWS

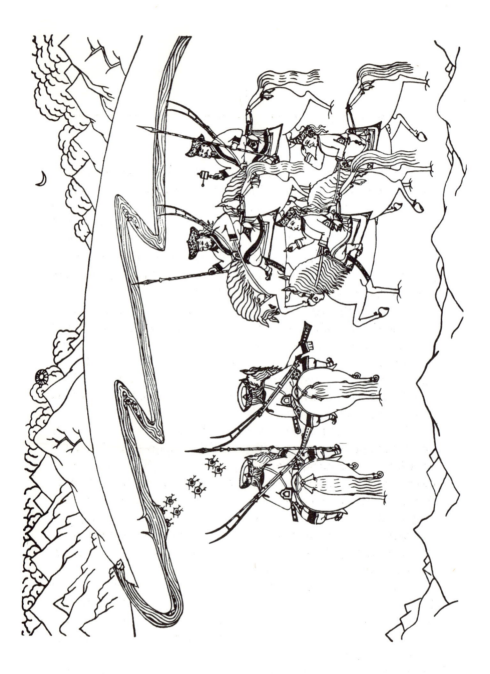

I

The tracks lead to the water's edge and end. None turns back. Like black marks made by a hasty pen on a new white page, the hoofprints write a record on the snow: the record of how a horse crossed the plain at a steady trot until he turned—or was turned —down the sloping bank of the river. There he faltered, tried to wheel, fought with the bit, and finally, driven by his rider's knees and flailing feet, went, with unwilling hooves that plowed long scars in the snow, to the water's edge and beyond.

No one of the band of riders who sit on their horses looking at those marks saw all or any of that happen. Yet each one reads the record unerringly. All is clear to the water's edge. Beyond that the tawny tide of Peacock Waters keeps its own secret, and the far bank—the distant hostile bank of Ngura—is half lost behind the snow that sifts scatteringly out of a cloud whose smoky streamers trail on the changing surface of the river.

The great gray horse of the Gurdu Lama left those tracks. He crossed the plain, sometime after the fall of snow dwindled to the vanishing point during the early part of the night, yet so near to daybreak that the few flakes powdering the dawn have not even frosted the black marks he left. Almost the riders hope to see the gray head, with the long pointed ears that are famous throughout the twelve tribes, pulling close to the far bank after the long swim. But there is only the surface of the river turning ceaselessly under the gray half-fog through which the snow still falls.

His rider was the Gurdu Lama himself—incarnation of the Holy Hermit of the Goddess of the Tiger's Den, Perfection of Wisdom, and Savior of the Twelve Tribes of the Shimdrok—who disappeared from the tiger skin yurt of the lama in the encampment of the Gurdu ombo sometime during the night: presumably at the same time the gray horse disappeared from the closely

3

guarded tether lines of the horse herd. The lama rode without saddle, for no saddle is missing, and did not stop at the water's edge to prepare for crossing in the orthodox manner with inflated "swim-bag" for a float, and the horse's tail for a tow. The tracks make that fact clear. The Gurdu Lama, trusting to the powers of the great horse, or trusting to his own destiny, good or otherwise, rode directly into the river.

Only the river knows whether he reached the far bank.

The river tells nothing to the men who, ranged in a half-ring, sit their horses and stare into the cloud-filled dawn. No one speaks or moves while that dawn brightens into day. All are waiting for the ombo to speak and the ombo, burdened with the mystery of his lama's disappearance—a disappearance that threatens tragedy—delays speaking to the last possible moment. If only the river or the far bank—half-hidden and hostile—would tell him what to say. Not only the men who ride with him on the chase are waiting, but soon all the people of the Twelve Tribes will be waiting to hear what account he has to give of the disappearance of his charge: his charge but their savior.

Even his younger brother, the second ombo in the Gurdu Great House, who sits his horse so close that their stirrups can touch, ventures no word but only waits for the ombo to speak. And the ombo, muffled in his wine-colored cloak of Lhasa broadcloth, sits on his white horse and looks at the tracks and the river; searching the gray fog, the brown waters, and his own dark thoughts for what he should say to all those who wait on his word of comment or command.

*   *   *

The Gurdu Lama was the third son of the family of Bang Thzang Yzimba, chief of the tribe of Rzachdumba: the third son and youngest, and maybe the least loved. For a time at least old Bang Thzang Yzimba had little love for the baby who had cost the life of his best-loved wife. And certainly the two older brothers paid scant heed to the wailing little creature. Only the servant woman who nursed him was completely satisfied, for she had lost her own child a few days before, and gladly took the insistent and rather fiercely hungry baby to her aching breasts. He had come into the world and life with death following hard after, but he clung to life with a fierce insistence, and thrived for all of a certain lack of care.

When the baby was three years old Yzimba suddenly discovered that he had the long, strangely tawny eyes of the wife who would ever be the best-beloved. The freely appraising tongues of the tribesmen—over-bold at times but limber with honest tribute of praise—had called those eyes the color of amber, but he remembered them as sometimes flecked with gold. Once indeed a frightened brave had called them tiger eyes, but Yzimba remembered them warmly golden. His sense of fatherhood had a sudden, if delayed, sense of satisfaction when for the first time he saw those eyes in the face of the dirty naked urchin who played in the sheltered lee of the tent. From that moment on he began to think and plan what he would make of his third son.

The eldest son would be chief of the tribe. Ah Ta already made his voice heard whenever the tribal council held session. The young men had commenced to follow his lead when either raiding or hunting. He would be the worthy son of Bang Thzang Yzimba, and would surely make the name of Bang Thzang and the tribe of Rzachdumba great; or at least well feared. His bold eyes and stubborn jaw promised that with complete finality.

The second son was a lama. Through no action, and by no choice of either his parents or himself, he sat in the Great House of Kong Thang Tsang in the lamasery of Labrang. When he was less than three years old omens, signs, the utterances of sorcerers, god-possessed, and horoscopes cast by the chief lamas of Amdo had picked him out as the incarnation of Aluk Kong Thang. Not the greatest lama of all the lamas of Labrang, but not the smallest either. Even in his teens the young lama promised well as a minor savior, and Bang Thzang Yzimba had gained in privilege and influence because of the second son who wore the yellow cap in the chanting halls of Labrang.

The third son could only become what his father chose for him; almost inevitably that was monkhood. Certainly Bang Thzang should give one son to the order. But seeing the child's sturdy body and the baby rage and daring that often flashed from those long yellow eyes, Bang Thzang Yzimba would sometimes wonder whether she of the amber eyes would have wished her only son to become a monk. His beads would lie idle in his slack hands while his thoughts were changed to memories in the far dreamland of time. And in that far land, again he would question what he would make of his third son. So the moment of final decision was put off from day to day, and the child grew.

Throughout those years, Bang Thzang Yzimba also began to change somewhat his own habits of worship. The tribe of Rzachdumba, and more particularly the family of Bang Thzang, had a special proprietary interest in the great Gurdu lamasery at Tahk Thzang Lhamo—the Goddess of the Tiger's Den. Three hundred years before, the great Rgyal-wo Wang of the Sohkwo had given the land to the first Bang Thzang Yzimba, chief of the refugee tribe of Rzachdumba. Then later the second Bang Thzang Yzimba had given the lamasery site, including the sacred forest and the cave of the Tiger's Den, to the Hermit whose holiness and power began the incarnation of the Gurdu Lama—Savior of the Twelve Tribes. Since that time the Gurdu Lama was in a special way the ward and protege of Bang Thzang.

But at this time the Gurdu Lama had been dead three years. The second son of the family of Bang Thzang sat in the chanting halls of Labrang. More and more Bang Thzang Yzimba began to worship at Labrang. The chanting halls and cloisters of Gurdu are just over the hilltop from the Rzachdumba winter quarters, and it takes five days of travel on horseback to go to Labrang. But five days of travel meant nothing to the chief of Rzachdumba when he could see his son, worship, and also trade to advantage. The men of Rzachdumba loitered in the market of Labrang and worshiped at its shrines. The gifts of the chief and his tribe were piled in the audience chambers of the dignitaries who manage the affairs of that greatest of the lamaseries; now still more great because Bang Thzang Yzimba was visiting his second son.

The lamasery of Gurdu, on the other hand, began to have a deserted look since the tribesmen of Rzachdumba no longer loitered in its squares and worshiped at its shrines. The wide barred gates of the lama's Great House had not been opened for three years, for there was no Gurdu Lama to come forth and bless the crowds. It seemed that soon there would be no crowds either, if the tribesmen of the other eleven tribes of the great plain began to follow the example of Bang Thzang Yzimba and his people.

Toward the close of the third year, during which the gates were barred and Gurdu mourned its Lama "honorifically gone into the zenith," the ombo, or manager of the lama's Great House, came out of his seclusion and made contact again with the life of the lamasery. The leading and aged monks met again and again, and the smoke of incense offerings and great burnings of juniper boughs flavored with butter, salt, grain and tea rose from the altars of the Great House, and climbed toward the cliffs and the arrow shrine of the Iron Mountain God set like a question mark written against the blue but silent heavens.

The monks met for special chants, and the dim recesses of the great chanting hall re-echoed to the insistence of their praying. Messengers, big with importance, rode the fastest horses of the Great House; setting out on journeys to consult the Wizard of Rebkong or the Savior of Kumbum, and came back charged with a weight of mystery, and with messages that were to unlock the future.

All the world knew that Gurdu was seeking its new Lama. Somewhere among the thousands of encampments and villages of Amdo there was a family whose three-year-old son would be revealed, not as son of his father but as the incarnation of the great Gurdu Lama—god revealed in flesh.

Did thoughts about his three-year-old son—he of the long yellow eyes and baby rages—ever enter Yzimba's mind when the news of this search traveled from encampment to encampment and from tribe to tribe? Certainly when the official delegation came to his encampment and entered his tent he showed no surprise.

The great Wizard of Rebkong, leader of the black hat sorcerers—he of the long hair of three fathoms length—after days of conflict with gods and demons, had proclaimed, through lips that dripped with bloody spittle and foam, that the Gurdu Lama would be found when one travels as the raven flies from the shrine of the Iron Mountain God toward the cave of the legendary Hor-ling. The very first time those instructions, which seemed to come more from the dead than the living, were followed the winter encampment of Bang Thzang was shown to be the only inhabited spot along the entire length of that imaginary line.

Between pauses in a special rendering of the Kangyur by his most sacred lips, the Savior of Kumbum had said that the Gurdu Lama would be found in a family of chiefs and lamas: child of a noble line.

So the rumors came to the encampment of the Rzachdumba

chief, even before the official delegation of the Gurdu Great House tied their horses at his tent door, and began the long round of consultation and negotiation that ended when little Shiang Cheung, still dirty and half clothed but with long yellow eyes that showed no fear, only a certain wary distrust of all strangers, was declared the Gurdu Lama of sainted memory, Aluk of the Goddess of the Tiger's Den, Savior of the Twelve Tribes, and the glory of the monk commune of Tahk Thzang Lhamo.

For four years after that day he continued to live at home, yet he was no longer a dirty urchin playing half-clothed in the lee of the tent, but a pampered darling clothed in satin and sure of the warmest seat by the fire and the tidbits of each and every meal. On the day when the passing of the old year makes way for the new, and he was reckoned seven years old, he was officially ransomed from his home by the Gurdu Great House and installed in the lama's palace. The Lama at last had mounted the golden throne, and the lamasery of Gurdu began to emerge from its long eclipse.

On the same day young Ah Ta took over from old Yzimba the actual leadership of the tribe, and took charge of the hundreds of cattle and horses presented to the family of Bang Thzang as the ransom price of the lama. Yzimba himself was now dubbed the Sacred Ram, and having fathered two lamas could look forward to days of peace and a position of influence, greater than mere authority, while he visited his son the Gurdu Lâma. Even the all-powerful ombo must give recognition to the person and words of the Sacred Father.

Ten years passed and the third son of Bang Thzang Yzimba had become the idol of the twelve tribes. He was godlike in his beauty and those tawny eyes enhanced his godlike stature and appearance. They too were yellow, though of a different shade from the sacred yellow of the Lama's cap and holy robes. Not a whisper of anything but praise and adulation sounded on the pilgrim path or in the cloisters of Gurdu, and the people of the twelve tribes were well content with their god.

To the thousands gathered on the day of the Wishing Prayer Festival he seemed more golden and glorious than any lama had ever been, and his presence and beauty dominated even the pageantry and drama of the Old and New Dance. The drama of the vanquishing of sin seemed but to bring its tribute to the golden figure on the golden throne. He moved his hands and thousands bowed to receive his blessing, he opened his lips and thousands strained to hear his benediction, and the eyes of the crowd, drawn as by a magnet, followed the gleam of those yellow eyes—but they called them amber.

The ombo watching both crowd and lama was well content.

Two years passed and some one had said that those amber eyes were tiger eyes. Even the lamasery censorship could not stop the tongues of the monks for it was common knowledge, whispered in the lanes and cloisters—even in the chanting hall itself—that the Gurdu Lama would not listen to the ombo, that he wanted his own way about many things, and that, for a lama wearing the sacred yellow, his ways were strange and his desires wild. Month after month the battle went on, and throughout the twelve tribes men talked in whispers of what the ombo said to the Lama and, increasingly, of what the Lama said to the ombo.

The Lama could never be changed. He was always and ever the lama no matter what he did. But the ombo—that was something different. Yet this ombo had held his position during the successive life-times of two lamas before he of the yellow eyes came. It was the ombo, or maybe his brother, who said those eyes were tiger eyes, and the members of the retinue in the Lama's Great House learned to recognize that gleam. Slowly the members of the monkish commune, the members of the lamasery council, and the members of the Great House household even down to the cooks and hostelers began to take sides in the contest that went on growing in intensity.

So matters stood at the time when the encampment of the Lama's household was set up near the bend of Peacock Waters. But that night the members of the Lama's Great House talked in whispers, and waited fearfully; wondering what would come, for in the tiger-skin yurt the Lama and the ombo spoke to each other as even they had never spoken before. What was it with which the ombo threatened the Lama, and what was the Lama's counterthreat? Those who thought they overheard dared not tell.

Yet the echoes of that quarrel shout in the ears of the riders who sit their horses and wait for what the ombo will say. Maybe those echoes are also in the words of the ombo when he at last speaks.

"No gain in trying to cross the river. We follow the bank

downstream. There are two places where we must look."

Without another word of explanation or instruction the men know they are to look for a dead lama, not a living one. Not far downstream there is a great whirlpool where the current filters through rocks that do their best to trap the waters of the sacred river. Below that pool there is a place too, where the river is filled with sandy islets and bars, and split uncertainly into a number of channels. At both these places the riders are to look, with fear and misgiving, for their lama. With the clink and rattle of snaffle bits the horses start to move off, and then suddenly the ombo speaks again.

"No need for all to follow the bank. My brother and I will follow the stream to the whirlpool. The rest of you cut across the plain to the sand bars at the second elbow of Peacock Waters. We will join you there for noonday tea. Build a smoky fire so we can find you."

The riders start, but the ombo and his brother still sit their horses, looking at the river that tells no tales however much they might wish it to speak.

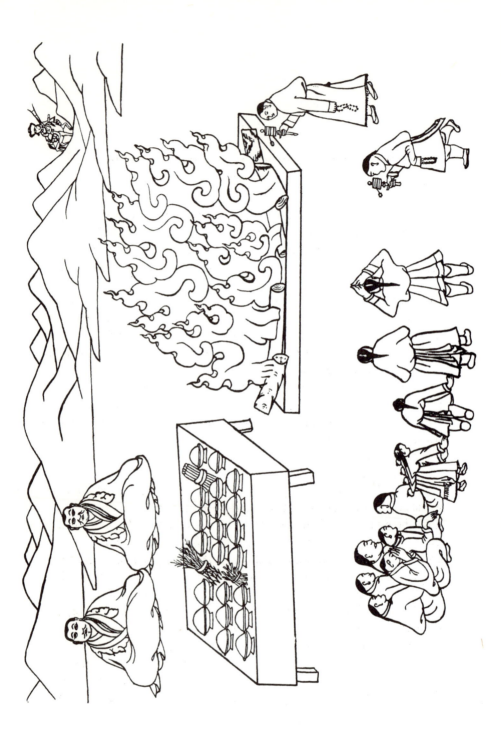

II

Thousands of tribesmen stand or sit in a circle on the plain of Ka-chu-kha that is spread from the mountains to the skyline like a great carpet—brown, russet and even lemon yellow—under a cloudless sky. Those who stand or sit so patiently come from many tribes: the nomads of the Shim-drok plains, Rong-wa from the land of farms where the waters that drain from the Tibetan plateau have cut valleys down to the level where crops will ripen, Sohk-wo from the "black tents," and even Goloks from the source region of Peacock Waters or from the foothills of Amne Machen.

The circle formed soon after daybreak, and monks of the lamasery police patrolled the circumference using their long whips with a heavy handed disregard of all in order to keep that circle wide enough. But now all motion has ceased, and the people of Amdo wait, with an expectancy that is like a breath held too long, for the "honored burning of the body of the Lama."

Daybreak finds the funeral pyre complete.

From their bivouacs, by hundreds of campfires, the tribesmen watched the movement of torches through the night, that showed how the members of the Gurdu Great House, and the monks of Gurdu, were preparing for the burning of their lama. They could count the torches that danced through the dark, and could speculate on the size of the pyre that was being made. But none anticipated a structure as great as that which daybreak revealed: timbers piled to the dimensions of a good sized house. In that half light the watchers nod to one another and say,

"The monks have done well to prepare a great burning of the Golden Lama who was drowned in the waters of the great river."

For he, the Golden Lama, has been drowned. He has not made the swim to the far shore. The ombo and his brother have found the body caught on the fangs of the rock ledges that bite at the

13

great whirlpool. They have taken it—just the two of them—to the tiger skin yurt, and around that darkened resting place the monks of Gurdu have watched unremittingly for ten days and nights; their unceasing prayers rising with the wind, seeming to die at sunset, but never completely stilled for they were chanting the final prayers and incantations that would follow their Savior "honorifically gone into the zenith."

During those ten long days the tribesmen were gathering: their tents and campfires spreading farther and farther across the plain until it seemed as if all of Amdo were gathered to do honor to the Gurdu Lama, now "honorifically gone into the zenith," and to offer consolation to the Gurdu Great House. Every one has brought his gift of condolence.

From dawn until long after dark the two ombos have sat to interview guests and receive gifts. Each one has made his speech: a mixture of eulogy, platitudes, shrewd bits of worldly reasoning and wisdom, and genuine sorrow and regret. And each one has presented his gift. The chiefs and men of wealth have brought herds of cattle, prize oxen, famous horses, rolls of Lhasa woolens, and ingots of white silver. Enormous wealth has flowed into the treasury of the Gurdu Great House. The bales of gift tea have been stacked in a pile that looks like the stock of a Sungp'an tea company, the ingots of silver have filled all the chests, so it is said, the rolls of cloth and brocade have made a wall at the rear of the guest tent, and the herdsmen of the Gurdu flocks are kept busy night and day looking after the droves of cattle and herds of horses that daily are added to their charge.

Enormous wealth is also spent each day. Hundreds, even thousands of guests are given tea and meals and portions of meat. Gifts of silver and semi-precious stuffs are made to all visiting lamas who have come to pray, not *for* but *because* of a fellow lama "honorifically gone into the zenith." Certain great and holy ones, the Wizard of Rebkong included, are retained to meditate and read the future and give oracular counsel as to what should be done.

The members of the Gurdu Great House spare no expense that the days of disposal should be a credit to their lama and to the honor of the lamasery. Hundreds of carrying oxen have made the trip to the nearest forests, at the head of the Zaru valley two days' journey away, and hundreds of timbers have been dragged across the Shami plain to make this great pile.

But the tribesmen have come not only to render their respects to the Golden Lama. They have come to trade, to discuss, to plot, and fill up with new excitement the round of their existence. Thieves sit around their tiny campfires on the fringes of the gathering and watch for their opportunity by night and by day. Chiefs meet to seal new alliances, adjust old differences; or maybe in some sudden flare of temper and voices new wars are born. Elopements are planned and assignations kept as men and women pass from one fire-side to another, and the plain of Ka-chu-kha is suddenly peopled with all the drama of Tibetan existence.

Yet in all the talk one question outranks all others in frequency, even after it has been answered a score of times. The nomads most of all are secretly unsatisfied, and, hands heavy on their swordhandles, are suspicious of their neighbors, the people of the valleys.

Why is the Gurdu Lama, Sum of Perfections and Savior of the Shimdrok who, mind you, are nomads, why is he being burned and not being given to the burial of heaven in which the vultures could come down on some high and holy mountain top and do a clean disposal in the preferred nomadic way?

The first official answer to this question seeps through the camp after the arrival of the Sohktsong Lama, who says that a lama who has been drowned by the malignancy of water must be burned by fire to overcome that evil influence. The Rebkong Wizard gives out the same oracular response, and the nomads perforce must be satisfied. But their suspicions will not rest, and they glare at their neighbors, the miserable Rong-wa, for burning is the method the Tebbu villagers employ in disposing of their dead.

But now all questioning and argument are at an end, and the tribesmen await the final scene: the lighting of the pile and the burning of the whole. Torch in hand, Musa the Moslem slips into the circle and advances toward the great pile of timber so skillfully laid. But Musa's steps are none too steady and even after he arrives at the pyre he seems to find difficulty in getting the flames of the torch to the kindling placed in the center of the pile.

He makes a number of futile attempts, even causing some derangement of the robes of brocade and yellow satin that cover the lama's body. A murmur of solicitude—a distressed whimper—passes like a gusty sigh across the circle. But the same superstitious terror; the same fear of committing some unnamable sacrilege which has forced the Gurdu Great House to retain Musa the Moslem for the task of lighting the pyre keeps every man in his place. No Tibetan—nomad, Rong-wa, Golok, Sok-wo, chief, "brave son," or miserable thief—however daring—would place the flame against that pile.

It is the right sort of a task for Musa the Moslem. Everyone knows him. For thirty years he has lived in the tents of the nomads and traveled from place to place, trading shrewdly but never largely. The men know him as liar, drunkard, and cheat, yet a good fellow for all that who at least has a proven courage. Many of the women know him too: a Moslem as shameless as the wildest Tibetan and one who sleeps with every willing wench he can find. Of the faith of Islam only shreds of the prophet's creed cling to him. Pork he will not eat, and in drunken moments he boasts of the sign of Islam he carries in his flesh. Those scraps of a hard and alien faith, together with natural courage and cupidity have armed him to do today's deed for which he is to receive one of the best horses from the famous Gurdu horse herd.

Musa has lived so long among the Tibetans, however, that their gods and fears are very close. Creed, courage, and greed need yet some further fortifying, and Musa, since long before daybreak, has been drinking from a score of jugs by as many campfires. The nomads have little to offer him, but the Tebbus know only one way of celebrating any event and have brought their celebration with them in little brown jugs. For once even they are generous. So his footsteps are uncertain and his hands clumsy and unsteady in the doing of his task, while the tribesmen hold their breath, and the Golden Lama, shrouded on his last throne, waits the tardy flames that climb so slowly from the wavering torch.

But the flames finally catch and Musa takes his zigzag course back to the edge of the circle. His work is done and for all of his greed, courage, and creed his face is yellow with fear. He needs, and indeed finds the largest brown jug ever packed in a Tebbu's saddle bag and for the time being the tribesmen see him no more.

They see only a pile of timbers that changes to a furnace as though hell itself had opened one of its gates on the Ka-chu-kha plain. The timbers of the pile begin to drip flame and ash and the roar of the fire is split into ragged fragments of sound by the crackling and the sharp explosions that shoot burning bits of wood into the air. The flames merge into a veil of bluish vapor that changes into smoke; blue and gray as it climbs toward the blue sky, but stinging and sharp as it swings around the circle, beaten to earth again by the wind that has risen with the beginning of the afternoon.

Then from the robes of the Golden Lama a black umbrella of denser smoke suddenly leaps toward the sky, and to the nostrils of the crowd, already stung by woodsmoke and ash, comes a heavy bitter odor: rank yet familiar. It is the odor that comes when a pot of meat boils dry over a fiercely blazing fire; the odor that curls up from under the branding iron; the odor of burning flesh. A half groan goes the rounds as the tribesmen at last sense the burning of the body of the lama. Something as stubbornly black as the smoke cloud above, sinks deeper into the glowing furnace in the heart of the pile and the flames play a wild game of tag over every timber and stick in the pyre until they are fused into a single pulse of heat that throbs to the beating of the wind. Never will the tribesmen of Amdo forget the burning of the Golden Lama. Certainly they should be satisfied that the flame lit that day has overcome the malignancy of the flood that killed him. The next emanation of the lama should be free from that baleful influence.

The roar of the fire fades into the chanting of the monks who pray louder than ever, and ashes, still hot but white like hoar frost, begin to sift over the crowd that waits on to see the very end. Yet they do not watch till the very end for horsemen ride past the distant campfires to the rim of the circle: horsemen on sweated horses and fully armed, though their hats come off to salute the holy burning.

The second question that has hidden in the thinking of hundreds then finds its way into speech, and men ask what they have not whispered heretofore.

"Why have not the men of Rzachdumba come to the burning of the lama who was the third son in the tent of Bang Thzang?"

But the question is half answered already by the coming of the riders, for the leader of the horsemen is Ah Ta himself; *de facto* chief and brother or half-brother of him who has now "gone to the zenith in flame." Yet Ah Ta, for all his hard riding, as the lathered condition of his great black horse attests, has come too late.

"But why late? Why late?" whisper some of the crowd as they

make way for the black horse.

Ah Ta never answers that question. Maybe he does not know the answer. Maybe the ombo knows, but from his assured seat in the midst of the monks of Tahk Thzang Lhamo he only gestures briefly in greeting and orders entertainment to be spread for the newcomers. And Ah Ta, for all the bold line of his jaw and mouth early settling into hardness, seems uncertain as to what he should do.

The wind takes great handfuls of ash and scatters it over the crowd that begins to break up. The fire has died to smoldering fag ends on the rim of the place where the pile had stood. Only ashes remain of the golden one who was third son in the tent of Bang Thzang. With a half sigh Ah Ta turns from those ashes, already scattering into the void of impersonal existence, and rides his horse to the guest tent where food is spread for himself and his men.

He has come too late to see the burning of his brother. The fact itself transcends its reason for being, or the solution of any problem it may raise. Quite simply he says to his men, and to all the world who may be listening.

"We have come too late to see the Gurdu Lama honorifically go to the zenith in flame."

III

Again the Gurdu Lama sits upon his golden throne. But this Lama is quite different from the lama of the yellow eyes. He also is the child of a noble house; the fourth son of the Thsa Ru Ma chief who rules the Thsa Ko near the Szechuan border. He too has been ransomed with thousands of cattle and great wealth at the age of seven, and has been brought to the Gurdu Great House to learn his lessons and grow up as a lama should grow. But still he is different. He learns his lessons well, even after the two old ombos died a year ago, for he is a meek and gentle lad.

His two older brothers are now the new ombos and his father too, the new Sacred Ram, lives in the Gurdu Great House. Thus the fortunes of two great domains—Thsa Ru Ma and Gurdu—are linked in his person. His sister has been newly married to the king of Ngawa and that marriage has added a third party to a combination of growing power and influence.

So the Lama sits upon his golden throne overlooking the pageant of the Wishing Prayer Festival, and to the hundreds of spectators packed in a dense ring and filling the square below to its very corners he is a god; golden in the sun; ageless and timeless in his perpetual existence and labors for the sons of men. At the very whisper of his name heads are bowed in worship, and aged tribesmen, with faces wrinkled against a too bright sun, count on a year of blessing because they again have seen the Gurdu Lama: Perfection of Blessing, and Savior of the Tiger's Den who by his presence makes the Wishing Prayer worthwhile.

To his brothers, two keen-faced young monks smugly conscious of power and influence as ombos of the Gurdu Lama, to the astute tutors and advisors of the Gurdu Great House, and to the envoy from Ngawa who has come to Gurdu for the first time, and who half hides his face in the folds of his mantle as he watches the crowds and seems to do sums on his beads, the young lama is neither all god nor all man, but a strangely potent pivot upon which great affairs will turn; smoothly or not at all. To his father, the Sacred Ram of nearly eighty years, he is utterly inexplicable: child of old age, god of an earthly sunset's last hope, and the source of a power and position that daily fill old eyes with a dazed wonder. What is he to himself? In all his twelve years he has never yet asked himself that question. Everyone tells him he is the Gurdu Lama. That is enough.

He does know however that as the dance of the Wishing Prayer Festival moves slowly to its foregone conclusion, he is bored, and the only relief from that boredom is afforded by the toys his brothers have placed in the folds of the yellow robes. The puppet Chinese pedlar with the tinkling drum is the best of all and his fingers spin the tiny drum handle to make the drum beat out its own faint rhythm. But his hands are held discreetly low, and the spectators in the square below think only of a rosary moving through hands like the palms of Buddha to count out a special blessing to their credit.

A number of those same spectators however, have ceased, seemingly, to think of the dance of the Wishing Prayer or the Presence on the golden throne. Five tribesmen and one equally dirty but slightly differently garbed stranger, linked in a sudden community of interest and fervent friendship, leave the square in a knot closely tied with Tebbu whiskey and argument, but pause to finish and settle their dispute where the wide steps of the great entrance to the square give them room to sit and a degree of quiet. Only the steady pounding of the great drums and the occasional blare of the trumpets can disturb their talk which throbs with heat and immediacy though it is of matters past and gone ten years and more.

"Why should he have been burned? Why?"

The old nomad gets no answer to his question from his companions and goes on.

"Some relics are covered with gold leaf and kept dry forever. Yes, forever. Or at least longer than men can live. I saw the relic of the former Kumbum Savior that was like a shrunken statue and has lasted a hundred years. Why not that? Instead they burned him like an ordinary Tebbu—a dirty miserable Tebbu."

His disgust can go no further and he seeks consolation in

Tebbu whiskey, wipes his lips, and whirls on the one nearest him with a sudden irrational rage.

"And you are the old devil who set fire to the pile. You— Chinese or Moslem or whatever you are, lama-burner—cooker of human flesh. The relic of the Lama, too."

Musa's old wits refuse to work, or at least to work in time, but one of the others speaks.

"Don't blame Musa. He was only a 'brave son' doing what someone had to do and no one else dared to do. You're a bold fellow, Musa. Brave son though you aren't a Tibetan."

"Yes, and took a great black horse for it too. Musa who even steals from the women he sleeps with. He earned a horse for burning the body of the Lama. Lama-burning Moslem, here, have a drink. You were drunk that day too. I saw you stumble and fumble when you burned the Lama. Burned our lama who should have been covered with gold leaf and kept a hundred years. Lama burning Moslem most miserable."

In a drunken haze that stirs like a stormcloud in the blast of epithet and insult, Musa's mind works confusedly toward some sort of self defense. Among all the things he remembers, or thinks he remembers, there is something that will refute all his tormenter says. Or is it something someone else told him that time when he was so drunk after the burning of the Lama? The men of Rzachdumba talked with him and told him many things that day. He had been too quick, or too early, or too something that day, they said. He remembers too, that they laughed at the horse he earned and said it wasn't enough. That too is part of the taunts that whip his mind and tongue toward some sort of speech. With the hot smart of whiskey in his throat that speech is released.

"The horse was a poor one. Big...yes, big...but..."

There was something about the horse he cannot remember.

"Big but not enough; should have been two," he announces with tipsy solemnity.

Drunken laughter rocks his hearers and they hold onto one another for support. It is just like a Moslem to quibble over price or quantity. But facts remain.

"Lama-burner, lama-burner."

They chant it in a mumbling chorus and pass him the jug in a spirit of drunken mockery.

"You burned the Golden Lama; the lama knows. Someone

should burn you," they shout with sudden rage.

But Musa's mind labors on, whipped by anger and spurred too by a bit of fear. He does not wish to be burned. And something he knows or remembers will save him. Something he dreamed perhaps. He wraps his arms around the shoulders of his fellows and their heads come together in sodden confidence.

"I did not burn the Lama."

So he assures them with all solemnity and waits for their agreement and approval. Instead their shout of tipsy incredulity lashes him afresh.

"I did not. I...there was only the hind leg of a cow...the lama's boot was a hoof..." His mind is flagging and confused images fight for preeminence. "His boots were cowhide...hooves so he was not burned."

Connected speech for Musa is ended, though the whiskey burns his mouth and throat again and again. Yet for a moment following that speech, in a flash of cold fear, he was completely sober. His five hearers stare stupidly at him but no question, denial, challenge, or even comment, comes through their slack lips. What they heard means dismemberment and slow death even for the simple hearing of it if ever the Gurdu Great House should know and catch them. But did they really hear it? As for Musa the root of his tongue tingles strangely for there the flesh would part if ever his tongue were torn from his mouth.

"Boots of cowhide...a hoof," he repeats owlishly.

His hearers begin to nod and then start the jug on its rounds. All further discussion stops for the jug is not more than half empty.

The Gurdu Lama sits on his golden throne but five at least of his worshippers are absent. They are sleeping off a bad dream that will sometimes haunt them when stories of the Gurdu Lama's wisdom and prescience are told.

Musa the Moslem gets drunker than he has ever been in all his drunken life. But when he comes to he suddenly reforms and like a devout Moslem who believes and follows the Koran he gives whiskey to those with whom he trades but leaves it alone himself, and, for his own profit stays clear-headed at their expense. Was he told, or did he see, what he in turn told that day of his last spree? He is not sure, but never again does he become drunk enough to know. Never again does he become drunk at all. It is too dangerous.

IV

The Gurdu Lama holds court in the big embroidered "four corners level" guest tent of the Gurdu Great House. The tent is pitched not far from the tiger skin yurt itself that dominates the encampment of Gurdu, for the Lama is spending the days of autumn with the tents. Those days when the threat of winter has not yet blighted the plenty that summer brings, and the herds are fat and sleek, are days fit for the enjoyment of the good things of life even for a lama. The fall visit with the tents of the Great House, when they are camped on the plain near Peacock Waters, is very much like a holiday, even for the Presence of the Goddess of the Tiger's Den. But today he holds court; seated on the cushions that make his throne, as the Enlightened One Himself sits on ten thousand idol scrolls.

By this time he is well used to sitting. The five years that have brought him to his seventeenth year have been filled with lessons of a Living-Buddha's life well learned. Even as he holds court, giving audience to the Lhasa pilgrims in the guest tent, he is indifferent to them and to their tales. Some day he himself will go to Lhasa—Gurdu Lama on pilgrimage giving and receiving blessing and sanctity—and will see all they talk about. Until then he is above the excitement that vibrates in their voices as they tell the wonders of their pilgrimage; more idol than human, more god than man.

He is well used to his throne. Desire for a saddle seat behind a pair of long gray ears never troubles him, and even this vacation in the autumn pastures of the Gurdu range brings little change beyond the vistas of hay fields that reach to the horizon under the wonder of an October sky, seen through the open door of the tiger skin yurt.

No one asks what he thinks. Maybe he does not think. It is

27

enough that he is impassive, aloof, sacrosanct. The perfect audience is when neither words are used nor thoughts employed. He is well trained in the giving of good audiences. This time he signifies his blessing, and the end of the scene, with the barest gesture of hands that are already dimpled at the knuckles.

Even the pilgrims who have seen Lhasa and all its wonders, including innumerable lamas, are impressed and take their departure silently. The ombo from his corner in the tent watches and is well content, and himself is a little too sleepy from good feeding to notice one of the pilgrims who hesitates in his going and seems about to speak. But there is no one to whom he can speak. The audience is over, though one might linger for a second helping of the food that has been spread lavishly. The Great House of the Gurdu Lama is truly a great house and does things well in the matter of hospitality—especially hospitality to pilgrims returned from Lhasa.

So the ombo does not see the one who hesitates in his going and seems about to speak. A few moments later he hesitates no longer but is gone. And if the ombo had seen him he would not have recognized him though he the pilgrim was once a member of the Gurdu Great House. That was in the time of the old ombo— the old lama too.

Five years ago at the time of the Wishing Prayer Festival the ombo was new enough to watch everything. He even knew that Musa and his companions were drinking and talking when Musa's companions at least should have been worshipping the lama on the golden throne. But he has ceased to look for anything but worship and adoration in the faces that turn toward the lama at festival time or in formal audience. Nor do his ears strain any longer to hear what he suspects anyone might be saying for now he suspects no one.

The power of the house of Thsa Ru Ma is completely dominant in the affairs of the Gurdu Great House. And the tripartite alliance of Thsa Ru Ma, Gurdu, and Ngawa more and more controls or makes a bid for control of the politics of all Amdo. Small wonder that the ombo—brother of the Gurdu Lama, brother-in-law of Mei Rgyal-wo king of Ngawa, and son of the Thsa Ru Ma chief—fails to notice one poor pilgrim who seems for a moment about to speak and then changes his mind and hesitates no longer in his going.

The audience is over and the guest tent is cleared. The Presence retires to the tiger skin yurt to watch his aged father—the Sacred Ram—tell his beads, to hear his brother tell about the successful business of the year both with the tents and in the lamasery of Tahk Thzang Lhamo, and to eat cubes of cooked tallow and suet rolled in sugar, for the lama is well entitled to the sweet and the fat—best of all foods.

The afternoon and evening chores of the encampment are done, and with the coming of the stars in the blue black curtain of the frosty night, all men are free to gather at their kettle fires for the evening time of food and story.

The pilgrims do not make up their evening fire for they have many fires where each one with his story of the place of gods, and his tale of the wonders to be seen at the Potala, is doubly welcome as guest and as pilgrim returned from a mystic argosy. One of them—one-time horse boy and packer of loads in the Gurdu Lama's retinue and now pilgrim returning after a long stay in Lhasa and other regions unspecified—has found old friends for all of the changes that take place in the lapse of twenty years. The old guardian of the Lama's horse herd shares a small but well ordered tent with his two assistants, and by their fire the pilgrim finds all the pleasure of reminiscence and comradeship. By the double glow of the fire and memory they go back into the past for the best things of life that always find their existence in the long ago, and there they find the perfect lama; the amber-eyed god of their early days.

"Ah, but he loved good horses and knew them, too."

The old herdsman's voice is bitter with regret that has not died in the passage of twenty years.

"Knew good horses and loved them. Remember the gray of the pointed ears? That was a horse. And how he could ride. He sat a saddle better than he sat a throne of soft cushions. Om mani padme hum! How he could ride! The lama knows—what a horseman!"

"Without a saddle too if he had to. Remember the time we broke the big sorrel and he was the first to ride it though the ombo told him not to? Ah, the lama of the amber eyes."

Only admiration is in the voice of the speaker. But the other assistant had memories of a different sort and maybe even more personal.

"Amber eyes it is true but sometimes they were tiger eyes. I am sure that when he was angry he could see in the night. Even a night as black as this one."

The pilgrim rises to his feet and going to the door curtain, throws it back to look into a night as black as the murk of Shin-rjechos-rgyal's dark realm. The dogs, too, are howling like demons in pain. They are all around the tent and he appears satisfied for he comes back to the fireplace and begins to talk, but draws three heads very close together with an imperious gesture before he speaks in low tones.

"In the Sera lamasery at Lhasa among the advanced initiates in doctrine and magic I saw one who had amber eyes. He was about the right age, too. I saw him several times too but do not know whether his eyes ever changed when he was angered. But they were amber-colored and just like those other eyes. Om mani padme hum. The initiate was just the right size too. It was wonderful."

Three faces stare stupidly at each other while the pilgrim again goes to the curtained door and challenges the night and his own uneasiness. He is back in time to hear the old herder speak. Yet in neither comment, question, nor refutation. The old man says with oddly inconsequential solemnity:

"Years and years ago I was at Labrang at the great festival when Ngura finally came back to recognition of the authority of Labrang. Officially the tribesmen of Ngura, who never surrender to anyone, tied their heads to Labrang as vassals once more—after thirty years of rebellion. When Ngura are in the saddle that is a sight worth seeing. But strangest of all: the most noted robber of all Ngura—Gar-bzang of Yak-hsi—rode a great gray horse that had long, long ears. Very long they were. The horse was five years lighter in color but the ears—the ears were just like the ears of the gray that the Lama rode. And it was five years later too."

Four pairs of eyes search each other, the fire, and the listening night just beyond the flapping tent wall for an answer to their questions. The old herder himself goes to the tent door, for the barking of the dogs has dwindled to a sleepy bickering, and the night wind seems weighted with questions that unseen questioners are asking. He comes back but half-satisfied and listens to speech even more guarded. One of his assistants has something to say.

"Musa—you know old Musa the Moslem? The last time Musa

was drunk he said something queer about the burning of the Lama. Do you remember what the Lama wore for boots at that time? Were they of cowhide? Yes, cowhide. Musa said something about a cow's hoof in the pyre and then changed the words "cow's hoof" to "cowhide boots." The Lama had worn woolen boots? But then Musa was very drunk. Yet it is very strange, he has never been drunk again since that day. Nor is he poor any longer. Musa the old rascal."

The fire dies to a faint glow but it gives no answer to their thoughts and the night is very dark. The pilgrim finds neither fire nor night to his liking. The one because it shows too clearly his face, and the other because it hides too completely what may be all too near in the dark. Haunted by that uneasiness he goes to his fellows.

And the Gurdu ombo never has a thought for the pilgrim who seemed to hestitate in leaving the guest tent, seemed to hesitate and about to speak but in the end left without speaking. Now he will never hesitate again for he knows he must not speak. But the wind has tongues.

V

Night is fading into dawn and the Drag Kar cliffs march into view with the growing light. Starlight showed the snowfields spread along the crest of the cliffs where the upper plateau begins; it also showed the snow-covered slope leading to their base. But the cliffs themselves were black in the shadow. Now with the dawn light they push the shadows aside and stand to greet the day: two thousand feet of crag and precipice fissured and scarred yet unscalable. In daylight they appear gray between the snows at their tops and the dark shadows at their feet. Of those shadows one is truly black: the yawning entrance to the Drag Kar Cave that remains black and threatening when all other shadow has yielded to the dawn.

The Drag Kar Cave—or caves, for the one entrance leads to a network of galleries—is a place of wonders: a place, too, of sanctity, for merit is to be gained by the doing of certain circuits or by worshipping in the cavern of the sacred images. There are many different passages; some low where a man must crawl, and some high-vaulted. In the dark there is the sound of running water, and the light of the torches shows black waters that boil in sink holes or along narrow channels of unknown depth. At the end of one cave is the Sea of Blackness and no one has been to the farther shore. Another cave is the Cave of the Dead where the bones of the earth creatures are piled. It is certain that the caverns lead under the earth to the very foundation of things—at least to the sources of the Sacred Kyi-chu and under the Place of Gods. The circuit of prayer along a path well-marked takes the time of three good torches, but one must have a guide for there are many turnings, and to be lost is the loss of life. Every year or so some pilgrim, seeking merit, disappears never to return by the entrance that leads to the underground world of wonders, fears, and shadow.

The monks of the Drag Kar lamasery, rising at dawn, habitually turn to that entrance that overlooks their cloisters, for the Drag Kar Cave is the principal reason for their lamasery's existence. Now, as always, to say their prayers they turn toward the mouth of the cave; black above the slope which is freshly white with a day-old fall of snow. Not a track nor a mark mars that white covering which is spread smoothly to the very edge of the opening.

As the monks chant the dawn is brightening into day. Sunlight, still pale and uncertain, creeps downward across the face of the cliffs and they change again: more scarred than ever. The sunlight reaches the upper edge of the opening and then seems to divide as it moves downward, tracing the irregular outline of the entrance, but it leaves the opening black as before. Suddenly that uniform blackness is broken. At the central point of the width of the opening, just above the white line of the snow, the sunlight catches on something bright. As though drawn by a pen dipped in gold, that something grows into a peaked figure; so the Jewel in the Lotus sits under the pointed vault that crowns the highest heaven; so the Enlightened One sits golden under the dark arch of the Gurdu Idol House.

The chanting of the monks breaks and ends in a confused shouting that in turn dies away, as they leave their praying and start climbing toward the mouth of the cave. The sunlight, moving downward to meet them, shows the unsullied whiteness of the snow across which they make fresh tracks as they scramble upward. And the watchers below—for not all have started upward—hear a faint and breathless shouting, as the acolytes and younger monks who are ahead come to a halt a short distance below the mouth of the cave, and wait for the older ones to catch up.

Robed and mitred as a lama: silent, immobile, except for a rosary that glides through one hand, the golden figure is just above them. When the older monks arrive there may be questions but before a dignity stern as a rebuke the acolytes are silent. As the other monks arrive a half circle forms around the mouth of the cave, but between that half ring and the sitting lama the expanse of snow is unbroken in its whiteness. Then the steward of the Drag Kar lamasery arrives at last and while the others are murmuring in ragged chorus "Om mani padme hum!" he is getting his breath to say at length—gaspingly:

"With reverence, but what is your Presence's title, and whence are you honorably come?"

The unknown one does not answer though his lips move to the rhythm of an inaudible praying. His robes and pointed cap gleam golden in the sunlight—robes rich and heavily trimmed with fur—but his face is dark and rather sternly set: the face of a middle-aged man who has met life head on, neither giving nor asking favors. Below the edges of the yellow cap his ears are long and heavily lobed: true lama's ears outlined against the gloom of the cave mouth.

The echo of the steward's question dies away and still the unknown one does not answer. Yet as though he had spoken the monks bow their heads. His will not to speak equally commands their assent.

"With reverence—the lama knows—with reverence."

They chorus softly lest the silence break too harshly abrupt. And then surprisingly he speaks.

"From Lhasa come."

Nothing is answered. Rather a thousand questionings are begun. Lhasa—the Place of Gods—is so far away: Lhasa beside the Sacred Kyi-Chu: Lhasa where eternal blessedness resides incarnate in the person of the Rgyal-ba Rin-po-che: Lhasa where the Potala stands like a great red and white cliff ordained as the dwelling place of the Savior of men: Lhasa the center of the world of belief and faith and the goal of the pilgrims' journeyings. From Lhasa he is come. But the fact, for fact it is; no one in his mind's last hidden corner of doubt questions that, the fact only poses the question with a new insistence. From Lhasa come—yes, but how?

Lhasa is three months' journey distant when the caravans take the higher caravan route, and those who go on foot and beg their way take a still longer time to make the journey. The season when the pilgrims arrive is months past and no lama has come from Lhasa this year. And the snow which has been spread so evenly to the very entrance of the cave for a day and a night is smooth and unmarred by tell-tale tracks. Equally the white snow in front of the lama and the blackness of the cave behind him suggest a strange answer to the question. "From Lhasa come, but how?" As though in answer to that silent question clamoring in the thoughts of all, the unknown lama raises his hand that holds the rosary, in a gesture that seems to include the cave, and the snow, and all their wonder and says,

"From Lhasa come: to sit here."

All signs of life leave that figure: life itself seems suspended. The lama sits in contemplation: in rapt absorption with powers and wonders beyond the knowledge of men. No one can tell if the golden figure even breathes though the eyes look out over the view on which the Drag Kar cave opens. Maybe they see beyond the mountains and the steppe. Maybe they see to Lhasa itself. Or maybe inward, backward remembering they see the dark underground world through which the Drag Kar caves go—no one knows where or how far.

But the monks of Drag Kar lamasery—the steward himself among the first—come to their knees in the snow.

"With reverence—with reverence—the lama knows—" they chorus softly as though the words were a prayer to the one who has come to sit there.

The sunlight is now stronger and more and more of the cave, as seen through the entrance, is visible. Yet in the space behind the lama, clear to the end of the first chamber or room, there is nothing to be seen of pack, kettle, or bedding: nothing of baggage or belongings such as ordinary mortals need on a journey from Lhasa to the Drag Kar caves.

Again quite suddenly the unknown emerges from his trance and speaks to the steward of the Drag Kar lamasery by name.

"Aku Sengi, you wish to know who I am? Go call the Gurdu steward who visits at your Great House, and when he stands here with you I will tell you who I am."

The acolytes run ahead with the message, and once they have left the vicinity of the mouth of the cave they whoop and yell as they race through the snow, but the steward follows more slowly, many anxious thoughts marking time in his mind as he plods along.

The visit of the Gurdu steward is somewhat of a secret, to the same degree that it is concerned with ecclesiastical politics, for he has come to the Drag Kar lamasery to pave the way for a change, maybe of allegiance. For at least two generations the little lamasery of Drag Kar has been subject to the control of the Labrang lamasery, but now Gurdu is seeking to extend its power, and there are those in the Drag Kar commune of monks who would willingly change masters and belong to Gurdu.

The Gurdu steward, traveling incognito, has come to the Drag Kar Great House. Only a few of the older monks know that the guest, for whom the very best is prepared, is the steward of the Gurdu lamasery. And yet that unknown one sitting in the entrance of the cave knows all about it and has sent for him. How does he know all that and why should he send for the man from Gurdu? Even as his feet stumble on the steps of the Drag Kar Great House guestroom, Aku Sengi's mind is stirred with an uneasy foreshadowing of trouble. He is one of those who are of the faction of Gurdu, and in half-felt fear he knows the menace of the unexpected: of all that which is not according to plan.

"With reverence honored guest—" he begins his speech while his mind still fights with its forebodings, and goes on to persuade the Gurdu steward to go back with him to the mouth of the cave.

Together, with frequent halts for breath or out of reciprocal politeness, they climb to where the lama sits golden in the sunlight. The monks still keep their places in a fairly regular semi-circle and by now the mutter of their praying has steadied to the rhythm of a chanting service. And the unknown one seems to have grown in permanence, in sanctity, and in power as though he were receiving worship as his unchallenged right.

"With reverence—we are here."

Aku Sengi has done what was asked of him. The Gurdu steward—now known to all the monks by his real title and position—has been brought. With the words—for all of his obedience—Aku Sengi ceased to exist for the unknown lama who only sees the Gurdu steward: looking at him with a stare that seems to go through him and accusingly onward down the long line of the years.

"Om mani padme hum!"

A prayer become faintly audible to the clicking of the beads, breaks off with words spoken to the Gurdu steward; spoken to the monk commune now gathered in full number in front of the cave door; spoken indeed to all who will hear in Amdo, the province of North-East Tibet.

"All who persecuted me and helped to drive me away are dead. The older ombo, the younger ombo, old Jamtso the teacher, the keb-khe of the year, and the steward before you: all—all are dead. I am Aluk Shiang Cheung. I am the Gurdu Lama."

The pronouncement admits of no discussion. It is oddly impersonal: an explanation of the workings of fate. The lama has ceased to look at the Gurdu steward. Almost it seems as if there were nothing more to be said. And then his eyes come back to those in front of him. As Gurdu Lama he suddenly has dealings with the Gurdu steward.

"You, steward of the Gurdu Great House, tell me, is my place ready? Or will I have to wait until my enemies of another generation die off?"

With the bare saying of the words one thing has been accomplished already. The Gurdu steward's mission to the Drag Kar lamasery has failed. That there are two Gurdu Lamas is unthinkable. That the one now enthroned in the Gurdu Great House at Tahk Thzang Lhamo should be false is unthinkable. But that the one who sits in the entrance of the cave of Drag Kar—come from Lhasa no one knows how—should be an impostor seems equally unthinkable. Let Gurdu lamasery do what it may with its two lamas. Any other lamasery is well out of the dilemma. For one more generation the lamasery of Drag Kar will remain anchored to Labrang.

But in the meantime let what blessing that may come from the unknown one's presence and benediction come. Let it fall in full force. It does no harm to worship and pray. The double row of monks bends and sways to the mutter of,

"With reverence—the lama knows—with reverence."

Only the Gurdu steward remains upright and unbending for he must go back to Gurdu where the managers of the Gurdu Great House await his return and the report he will bring. He dare not bow to this lama—Gurdu Lama that he calls himself—and go back to the other lama and his omboes. And yet—. It is true; what the unknown one has said. All are dead who took sides against Aluk Shiang Cheung the former lama. Dead before their time, too. Does death follow in this lama's glance? Straight and unbending, but with stiff lips that can hardly form the syllables of a prayer, the Gurdu steward sits and waits the pleasure of his host, waits most of all the will of the figure throned in the mouth of the Drag Kar cave. That figure may not be the Gurdu Lama, but the Gurdu steward dares not move without his dismissal lest an unknown curse fall upon him.

War has begun, and the words "I am the Gurdu Lama" are the declaration of that war.

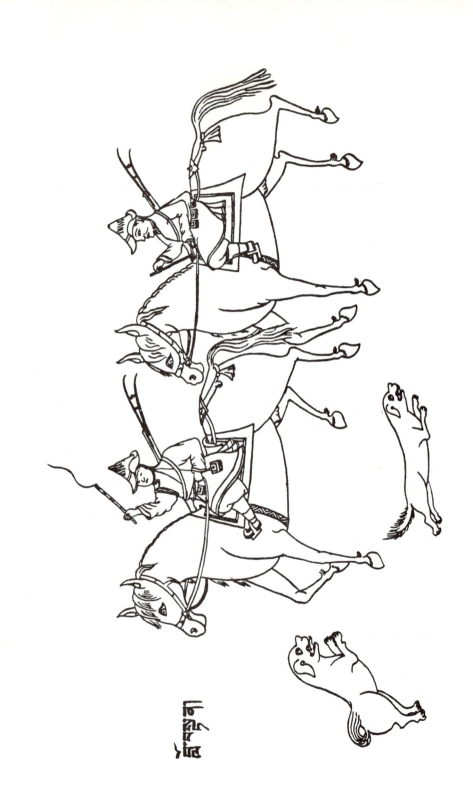

VI

Two riders break through the rim of the encampment and move at a steady trot across the empty space within the circle of the tents. They sit at ease, slightly sidewise in their saddles and back to back, that the heavy whip handles whirling at the end of the tie ropes which they swing around their heads like spinning halos, may furnish equal protection on both sides. On the circumference of that moving island of safety half the dogs of the encampment lunge and snap, driven by the deepest instincts of their being but held in a sort of enchantment by the whistling ropes that pass over their heads with the threat of more blows.

The riders laugh and tantalize the dogs with taunts, and by trick of wrist and shoulder bring the flying whip handles close to the bolder muzzles in the pack. So occupied and well-heralded they cross the encampment of Rgyal-wo Wang and come to a halt, not in front of his tent or tents, but in front of the small yurt and tents of Aluk Shiang Cheung, who camps with his patron and protector—Rgyal-wo Wang king of the Sokwo.

Even with such patronage he is still only Aluk Shiang Cheung, though three years have passed since he sat in the entrance of Drag Kar cave and proclaimed himself Aluk Shiang Cheung—the Lama of Gurdu. He has won much during those three years.

On that first morning, sitting golden in a shaft of sunlight, he won a hearing for the words "I am Aluk Shiang Cheung—I am the Gurdu Lama." And with the saying of those words he won fear, hate and belief: fear in the heart of the steward of the Drag Kar lamasery: fear lest he and his faction that had contemplated alliance with Gurdu were already too deeply involved to extricate themselves from an association that promised trouble: fear too, in the heart of the Gurdu steward who sat unbending yet daring not to leave until dismissed. Fear in his heart and also hate toward the unknown one who brought such a threat to his position and very

41

life. He was one of those who had been of the faction of the ombo and the words of the threat hung over him like a blow half struck. From that day on hate, come of fear, was to be one of the controlling motives in the policy of Gurdu toward the one who sat that morning in the cave of Drag Kar and announced his claims.

He also won belief. Of one thing the monks of Drag Kar lamasery—all the monks who were bowed in a semi-circle around the entrance of the cave—were fully persuaded. The one who called himself Aluk Shiang Cheung, lama of Gurdu, might or might not be the lama of the Tiger's Den as he asserted, yet no one questioned the truth of something he had not even said, much less asserted. All believed implicitly that he was come from Lhasa by the subterranean route in the unexplored galleries of the caves of Drag Kar, that extend most assuredly through the underground land of fears and shadows to the Place of Gods itself. That the manner of his coming was supernatural was certain. Before the day ended the legend was already full-size in the minds of those present. Even the strongest adherents of the Gurdu official policy and the bitterest haters of the unknown one seldom attempted a refutation of that legend. It grew with embellishments but always the untrampled snow in front of the cave door and the unknown one's complete lack of equipage were the foundation facts that could only be accepted as conclusive.

He won his claim and by his presence—so full of mysterious dignity—the right to the name Aluk Shiang Cheung. He had said, "Aluk Shiang Cheung—lama of Gurdu" and although at the end of three years he had not won acceptance for the last half of that statement, he was called Aluk Shiang Cheung from that first day. For his enemies the only alternatives for that name were epithets, but for his adherents all the power and position of the Gurdu Lama were implied in it, and for the rest it was the name of a mighty lama. So he won the name Aluk Shiang Cheung although he did not yet sit on the golden throne of Gurdu in the Great House of the Goddess of the Tiger's Den.

He won also wealth. That first day he had nothing. He asked nothing. He merely sat in the sunlight: a figure impressively impassive: a being needing nothing. Finally at the repeated invitation of the steward of Drag Kar he rose and walked across the yet untrodden snow—for no one had dared crowd too close—and went down to the Drag Kar Great House guest room. The single set of tracks leading outward in the snow, which he left, became also a part of the legend of the Aluk Who Had Come—whether he were the Gurdu Lama or not.

Installed in the guest quarters of Drag Kar—the steward of Gurdu was already gone in consternation, riding to take the news to Gurdu—the newcomer was found to possess nothing beyond his rosary: not even a bowl. Yet he drank his tea out of a precious blue Ming bowl and ate with ivory chopsticks. A young acolyte was self-installed—no one could remember afterward just how— as servant of the lama. From someone else there came the gift of a roll of paper-thin silk, yellow as a lama's hat. On his own initiative the acolyte cut the silk into squares, re-cut each square from corner to corner into two triangles and knotted them together to make the regulation scarf of blessing. The owner of the Ming bowl knelt to receive the first scarf: a presentation made with graceful movements of mystic import after prayers and blessing blown up- on it. And then he went to tell a curious expectant audience the sensations of power and ecstasy he experienced; sensations well worth even a Ming bowl. After that the gifts came even faster and still the lama seemed only to pray and wait, asking nothing.

The legend grew, for the newcomer's oddly shaped eyes seemed to promise strange things when they rested on each one who knelt to receive a scarf of blessing. The legend grew, and by dawn of the second day had traveled far, for on that day the little acolyte was kept well busy making scarfs and putting away gifts.

At the end of five days Aluk Shiang Cheung set out for Lab- rang. He rode an excellent horse superbly equipped, and the aco- lyte rode another one of less value; but serviceable and strong. The baggage of a lama traveling on a journey of somewhat indefinite duration was loaded on two pack mules. During the preparation for the start the lama did nothing, yet silently commanded and gained the service of all in the loading up. Once some distance down the trail, however, he ordered a halt to reload the mules and himself reroped the loads with amazing strength and skill: using intricate ties and hitches his companions had never seen. The loads stayed well balanced all day and to the legend of the One Who Had Come there was added another chapter.

In Labrang Aluk Shiang Cheung seemed to be merely waiting: unwilling to install himself even after a house had been offered to him; unwilling also to leave. Yet while he lingered worshipers

came and his wealth increased. But certainly he was only waiting.
Waiting for what ? For messengers from Tahk Thzang Lhamo or
for the coming of the men of Rzachdumba, when they come with
their chief to visit and worship Aluk Kong Thang Thsang? Yet
he never asked anyone for news of the region of the Twelve Tribes
of the Great Southern Plain, and he never paid Aluk Kong Thang
Thsang a visit all the time he stayed in Labrang.

Then one day he seemed to have tired of waiting and he asked
the acolyte, as he poured tea into the Ming bowl,

"Where is your home, little resembling one ?"

"The encampment of Rgyal-wo Wang, king of the Sok-wo,
with respect," answered the acolyte with the palms of his hands
outspread.

The next day Aluk Shiang Cheung left for the encampment of
Rgyal-wo Wang, king of the Sok-wo.

He gained wealth and was well-served. Rgyal-wo Wang gave
him the gift of a yurt, a hundred sheep, and twenty *mdzo-mo*,
milch cows, matched in color—golden red beauties with hair like
silk. The tribesmen of Nguru passing through the region of the
Sok-wo gave him twenty *mdzo*, carrying oxen, similarly matched
in color. Thereafter the only oxen or milch cows he would receive
as gifts had to be of the same color, and his milch herd as well as
caravan of baggage animals quickly became famous. Sheep, cattle,
Lhasa woolen cloth, and bar and ingot silver came to him as gifts
in very fair quantity. Yet horses were his real interest and he received gifts of the best horses from many regions—Si-ning pacers
and tough Golok ponies among them. He and his party were always superbly mounted.

The most surprising gift of all was a great gray horse that came
from the Sok-tsong chief's famous horse herd. Yet Sok-tsong was
one tribe completely under the dominance of the Gurdu Great
House and the Ngawa king. No one seemed to know just whence
and how the horse came to Aluk Shiang Cheung but the fact
remained that he received one of the famous big horses of Sok-
tsong: a great gray with long, shapely, pointed ears.

He was well-served. He sought no ombo to direct him but
directed his own affairs, using the acolyte as a sort of under-stew-
ard, and his affairs, even apart from gifts, prospered. His servants,
both men and women, were well-fed, well-clothed, and well-
mounted. The tribesmen of North-East Tibet will render good

service if those three items are adequately taken care of. Discretely smaller than the establishment of his host and patron, everything he possessed was yet of the best and his prestige kept pace with his "appearance": his reputation resplendent as the swank which characterized him.

Lama without lamasery, without Great House, without a generally recognized doctrinal status, without even an official name, he yet prospered amazingly. He had great and strange powers. His horoscopes were never known to be wrong. Sometimes indeed they were misunderstood, for they were always mysteriously hard to understand, but they were never wrong and men debated his least utterance as though they were part of the Sacred Writings. Unexpected meanings revealed themselves to those who pondered well his sayings.

He forecast correctly the defeat of Labrang in the war with the Moslem warlord of the Koko Nor at a time when every other Tibetan oracle prophesied victory. He forecast to the day the return of the annual pilgrim caravan from Lhasa with additional information about the condition of the trail and weather conditions in Golok country that were amply confirmed by the stories the pilgrims told. He prophesied the "honorific passing into the zenith" of the Rgyal-ba Rin-po-che—the Dalai Lama himself—the very year it took place. He told of the coming fall of the Hutuktu of Urga, in outer Mongolia and the establishment of secular rule and the Mongolian Republic months before it took place: making the prophecy in Mongolian faultlessly spoken, to the amazement of all who heard. He ordered the journey of Rgyal-wo Wang to the medicine house of the outlanders in Lanchow, the capital of the Chinese province of Kansu; prophesying success and healing, and the prophecy was fulfilled in every detail. So, too, for minor forecasts about sickness, death, birth, strayed cattle, and the unnumbered problems of life that can only be solved by being referred to the lama: he gave answers that were often mysterious— too full of wisdom for comprehension—but never wrong, and the hearers murmured a phrase once trite as repeated prayers but now suddenly new with a growing conviction,

"The lama knows—only the lama knows."

So the legend of the One Who Had Come grew to be the legend of the One Who Knows.

He effected miracles of healing; ordering strange new treatments that were highly successful. He stopped the plague of rinderpest among the Black Tent tribes by an expedient—the letting of blood and the polluting of the waters—that shocked every religious and community taboo, yet was so successful that it was soon adopted by every tribe living north of the knee of Peacock Waters. Several cattle sick with the disease were taken to the source of the stream which watered the entire range of the tribe, and at that place their throats were cut and the blood let flow into the stream. For some days most of the cattle of the tribe seemed somewhat unwell but there were only a few deaths and the plague of rinderpest disappeared. Great was the power of Aluk Shiang Cheung.

To the yurt of Aluk Shiang Cheung—lama of power and influence—came guests of every kind and degree. In addition to tribesmen from all the northern tribes, and individuals from among the southern tribes as well, Bodpas from Lhasa came to talk to the Aluk in the strange and almost unintelligible dialect of Lhasa. Mongols from the Ordos to talk to him in Mongolian. Chinese traders to talk in Chinese. He understood them all. Yet the lama, who spoke many languages, seldom spoke and never asked questions. But the questions he never asked were answered by those who talked with him—or to him. They told of happenings near and far, they told the news, and they told the rumors that echo and re-echo in men's minds until they become fact. They told all, to the one of the strange eyes who seemed to understand all, and then they went away convinced that they had said nothing; only received a blessing of mysterious value.

Among the guests who came there was, however, one noticeable omission. Few if any chiefs ever came to the yurt of Aluk Shiang Cheung, and none from the Southern Plain. An official visit involved too much. The powerful alliance of Gurdu, Thsa-ru-ma, and Ngawa dominated the politics of Amdo. Yet there was not a chief this side of the Goloks who had not had some trustworthy agent or representative make a call—a call unofficial and yet always respectful and properly accredited with gifts.

But never before have guests come of such importance as the two riders who cross the encampment of Rgyal-wo Wang with such an assured contempt of the dogs, and dismount in haste and a sense of great importance in front of the yurt of the Aluk. They are messengers to announce the arrival of Ah Ta, chief of the tribe of Rzachdumba, who has journeyed far to make this visit.

The arrival of the chief and his men is an occasion of the wildest confusion throughout the whole of the encampment of the king of the Sok-wo. Scores of horsemen beat off the dogs, answer greetings, accept invitations, and little by little scatter to the firesides and the tetherlines of the encampment. The men are guests drinking tea by a hundred hearth fires: the horses stand and wait patiently until their time for grazing shall come: the chief of Rzachdumba, Ah Ta the bold, makes his obeisance to Aluk Shiang Cheung.

Gifts—a square brick of the whitest silver—it should be good for it has 'Sterling' stamped on it and the seal of the Bank of England: Lhasa broadcloth, furs, and yellow brocade; all displayed to the best advantage and speaking plainly in the silence.

Gestures—the wideflung palms and bent back of Ah Ta the bold before he took his seat cross-legged on the rug in front of the lama: the scarf of presentation held stretched from hand to hand, first of Ah Ta and then of the lama, and the final exchange of the two scarfs; then the symbolism of benediction and the scarf of blessing looped around the chief's neck, which was the lama's complete answer to all that the gifts have said.

Words—the murmur of prayers that never falter as the lama searches with his strange regard the face in front of him and finally speech, at least articulate, from the other one.

"Lags-so—the lama knows—lags-so."

So Ah Ta acknowledges the bestowal of grace and the permission to speak.

In reality there is little enough said and sometimes the silence seems heavy with a thousand things unsaid. Again they talk in polite guarded phrases of travel, the weather, the health of the herds, and the date of the next move for all the tribes. Only once do their words seem to approach what all present are thinking.

"You have come a long journey—five days is it not ? Yet for three years I have waited to see the Rzachdumba chief."

"Lags-so. The lama knows," answered Ah Ta. "And I—I have waited for this meeting twenty-three years."

Ah Ta, chief of Rzachdumba, leaves in a haste seemingly greater than when he came. In his silence no one can read what are his thoughts of Aluk Shiang Cheung the lama who—great though he may be—has yet to establish his claim to the lamaship of Gurdu. But at one time in the past the lama of Gurdu was his brother, or half-brother—sons of Yzimba both of them.

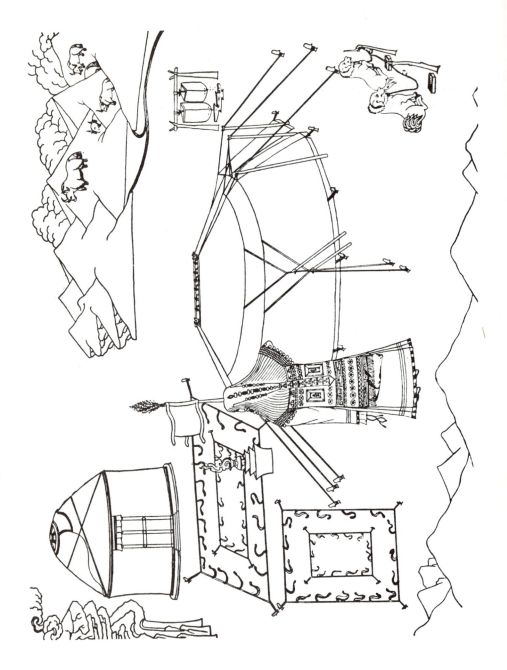

VII

In the summer encampment of Rgyal-wo Wang, king of the Sok-wo, it is only the distance of a scant hundred paces from the doorway of the great home tent of the king to the yurt of Aluk Shiang Cheung. Yet they are worlds apart.

The tent is a low black rectangle that hugs the ground: the guy ropes stretched like the claws of a many-legged creature holding hard against the wind. It seems to sprawl in careless mood: always more open than closed, and the debris of the habits of nomad life are littered within and without. Felts, raincoats, sheepskin garments, and pack covers hang on the long guy ropes; fuel baskets and milk pails are scattered near the curtained doorway, and directly in front of that entrance the great churn is placed throughout the day that sunshine may hasten the coming of the butter. In addition to the coming and going of guests and serving women, warriors and children, calves, lambs, and puppies tumble under the caves or nap in quiet corners. And over the flat roof drifts a cloud of smoke that rises through the central smoke vent or seeps through the meshes of the yak-hair cloth.

But the yurt stands a white cone against the sky; aloof and self-contained; having nothing to do with life. Even when the lama is honorably enthroned within the door is generally shut, and no trace of smoke hangs above the circular skylight. A low picket fence around the yurt keeps even stray puppies or calves at a respectful distance from the place where the lama meditates, while through a half-open doorway comes the sound of praying.

On a day deep in summer just as dusk begins to fall the daughter of Rgyal-wo Wang stands at the tent door and stares at the yurt with a strange intensity in her look. The lama is not even there. No murmur of magical incantations breaks the stillness and the door of the yurt is closed. The lama is far away riding alone on his own concerns.

Looking at the yurt she has stopped her churning, and a servant women, coming from within the tent, takes the handle of the churn dasher from her slack hands. Wan Chen Mtso moves aside, still staring at the yurt and busied with thoughts that wander in some far place, while without conscious direction her fingers feel under her right ear for an earring that should be there and is not. Heavy with gold and coral and pointed with a tiny bead the color of pigeon's blood, the other pendant still hangs by its cord wound around the left ear but her fingers find neither cord nor pendant under the right one.

The lama took that from its place as he leaned from his horse in the dim half-light of the break of day. Wan Chen Mtso had led his horse from the tent door to beyond the rim of the encampment, as the daughter of the tent should do for an honored guest, for the lama had taken his early tea with Rgyal-wo Wang before leaving. As she let her hand drop from the bridle, setting free his horse, the lama made that swift gesture and her earring was gone. His horse, too, was gone in an instant: that great gray of the long ears that pulled so savagely at the bit, and his rider had said no word.

But Wan Chen Mtso staring so hard at the yurt knows where and when she will get her earring back. It is only a token but a token of deliberate purpose and plan. The reality is something burning between the imperious unpredictable soul of Aluk Shiang Cheung—lama directing his own destiny—and the pride and passion of Wan Chen Mtso, only daughter of Rgyal-wo Wang.

There had been no token on that day of fickle sunshine and constant wind when they had first been together some months previously, as there had been no sign between them throughout the months that had gone before or those that have since passed.

He had sat times without number by the hearth fire in the great tent; sipping tea, talking with the changing coterie of those who make up Rgyal-wo Wang's small court, or just silently letting his thoughts keep him company. Often the daughter of the tent had kept him company too as she tended the fire or beat out the butter. Sometimes, too, she had poured his tea; passing the bowl to him with both hands.

"With respect," she had said.

But her eyes—did they always match her words? His half unwilling gaze would follow her—famous beauty of the Black Tents—with privileged stare of a lama who was above question. Sometimes instead of reverence it was pride, and the answer of a woman well sought after, that had returned that look. Again and again she had led his horse—"with respect"—to the rim of the encampment as the daughter of the tent should do to speed him on his way. Or she had spread a rug—"with reverence"—for the lama, but the gesture was charged with sudden intimacy for the man.

That had been all until the day they met alone on a wind-swept hilltop. She had made company for the servant girl in watching the sheep but in the midforenoon the servant girl had left on some excuse. Wan Chen Mtso well knew, however, that it was a rendezvous. But the girl would be back at the campfire before dark so it had made little difference to the daughter of Rgyal-wo Wang. She had consented readily enough and had laughed at the haste and the ill-concealed eagerness the girl had shown. But the knowledge that it was a tryst that had called the other away had made her own pulse quicken just a little. Something stirred in her: though the sunshine was fickle, yet spring was in the air, and the ground warm even if the wind did still moan of winter.

The great gray horse of Aluk Shiang Cheung came up the hill with a sudden rush that took her by surprise, though she got to her feet in time to speak a welcome and hold the horse's head as the lama dismounted. He had come like the sudden rush of the wind, so she had no time to change back into her great sheepskin coat that was spread fleece inside out in the sunshine. Her wine-colored raincloak of Lhasa broadcloth was strapped around her in somewhat incidental fashion leaving shoulders and even breasts bare. Yet as she stood to hold the horse she covered them with the long sleeve out of respect to the lama who had come.

He was Aluk Shiang Cheung, yet except for the yellow facing of his lambskin coat he was attired as a layman: a layman of distinction—fox fur hat à la Golok, rifle on his back and sword tucked crosswise in his girdle. So he frequently rode far and recklessly alone on his own concerns, rode as a lama never rides, trusting for safety—not to his lamahood—but to his gun and the speed of his horse.

Wan Chen Mtso hobbled the horse and then came back to do the duties of a hostess to the unexpected guest at her fire.

"I saw your smoke from far down the valley and thought it was a herder's camp."

"Where are the others? Are you alone?"

His voice changed slightly in saying the last words and he slipped his shoulders out of his coat, letting it fall around his waist the better to get out his bowl and set it by the fire.

"Alone, with reverence," she answered. "Alone, with respect, but Yok-mo will return before it is time for the sheep to start back to camp."

"Ah, Yok-mo." The lama's voice was casual. "What is she doing away from the fire?"

Wan Chen Mtso was fixing the lama's bowl for the pouring of tea—a heaping spoonful of dry white cheese of the fineness of coarse sand: a spoonful of roasted barley flour covering the cheese and patted down in the bottom of the silver lined bowl; shavings of butter—many of them—curled into that same bowl set by the fire: so she prepared the bowl for the pouring of the tea. And then her left hand held palm out in mid-air with respect while she poured from the ladle the milk tea of a nomad's kettle.

"With respect—the lama knows—with respect. Will the Presence partake of tea? And here, too, is boiled meat."

She seemed not to have heard his question and rocked back on her heels to work the goatskin "fire-bag."

"What is Yok-mo doing on a day like this?"

He repeated the question as he picked up the bowl and then bowed his head against the smoke that swirled and flattened with the wind. The girl ducked from the path of the smoke and they were closer together than they had ever been. She answered.

"What would she be doing on a day like this? What would she be doing when she is with the one for whom her flesh burns?"

There was only silence heavy with things that could not yet be said to answer that, and as the smoke lifted each one stared into the day that was. "A day like this" she had said. The day was blue and golden: while the last breath of winter fought a losing battle against the warm birth of summer.

The campfire was on a hilltop but actually half hidden in a hollow on that top. Only the far mountains and the sky were visible from where they sat beside the fire. Those mountains were yet covered with snow, but close around them the new green grass was halfway up through the clumps of old winter hay, and the earth, released from the grip of frost and suddenly warm, gave back the fickle sunshine as a somewhat constant heat. No wonder the girl had spread her great sheepskin coat out to the sun and wore only the wine-colored cloak strapped to her so as to leave her arms and shoulders bare.

Her hair hung around her face in an irregular bob behind which her eyes waited in ambush.

Suddenly she knew that she wanted him with all the intensity of her youth of eighteen summers. She wanted Aluk Shiang Cheung whose smooth untanned shoulders seemed almost golden to match his cloak, made and worn in layman style but yellow, too. Those shoulders were far lighter in color than her own sunburnt back and she wanted to set her teeth in them or at least feel them gripped within her half-closed fingers. She wanted Aluk Shiang Cheung and the enormity of that desire made anything permissible.

She spoke in a choking voice.

"What would you be doing with the one you chose on a day like this if you were alone? Alone."

In the saying of the last word her eyes leaped from ambush and fought a strange battle with his own, and her breasts were no longer covered out of respect for his lamahood.

She was never to know how old was the desire that flamed to answer hers. He was a man of strange and persistent reticences. She never knew what he already felt when the great gray came to a halt beside a fire where she sat alone. She never knew whether he had even ridden to find her when he heard the plans for the day discussed as he drank his early tea, or whether it was something that had flashed into sudden gigantic, whirlwind, existence and power when she had torn his lamahood from him with the use of the pronoun you—thrice repeated, and then had challenged all the new manhood uncovered within him with the word—alone.

She was never to know. But in that half hidden hollow where the wind passed overhead and the earth under them changed the fickle sunshine to constant warmth she was amply content to give herself to him and to a desire that well matched her own.

Afterward he was still the lama. If she had told he would have still been the lama just the same, for "only the lama knows." Against that sure knowledge the testimony of anyone—even of the senses—is illusion. Indeed, in the months that followed Wan

Chen Mtso even wondered herself whether the testimony of her own senses was not illusion, for all was as before. Never by look or word did Aluk Shiang Cheung recall those moments on the hilltop. It might never have been. Yok-mo coming back had found Wan Chen Mtso alone. Had she not been alone all the time?

At a point midway in the passage of those months Ah Ta the Rzachdumba chief came to pay his long delayed visit. And after the visit the days passed as before.

Often Wan Chen Mtso wondered about the future of the Lama Shiang Cheung. She well knew that as a recognized lama he might even take a wife—several wives indeed—and still remain a lama. In fact no act of his could ever change that. A lama remains a lama until his death, though his prestige may suffer because of his acts in defiance of the rules of the monkish order. A lama is not a lama because of something studied, gained or merited, but the simple fact of being is his final argument for, and supreme claim to, lamahood. Even if she had told and had been believed he would still have been the lama.

Aluk Shiang Cheung was in a sense still only a claimant playing for great stakes. He had won as yet only a tentative status. Perhaps that was why he never by word or look recalled those moments on the hilltop. Perhaps—but Wan Chen Mtso too was proud, and though in the night she dug her nails into the palms of her hands with longing for the feel of his shoulders, yet she too made no sign even when she poured his tea for him in the black tent and they were alone.

Then in the half-light of daybreak Aluk Shiang Cheung leaned from his horse and with a swift sure gesture—like a blessing bestowed—took her earring and was gone. Gone to ride in his wild bold way on his own affairs throughout a long day, but sure to return to the yurt at night.

Because of that Wan Chen Mtso stands in the doorway of the tent and stares at the yurt, for it is time soon that the lama be getting back. Then she will go one hundred paces to another world, and will spend the night in the strange half-mystic place—the white yurt that is so far removed from life. She will walk that distance—only a hundred paces—to win back her earring: jewel of a king's daughter.

Other women go to tents or to secret sleeping places on the

rim of the encampment for such trysts: to tents to find a man—to tents where the debris of a nomad's way of life is scattered all around, or to some warm lair where furs and a felt raincoat make for shelter right among the herds. But she will go to a lama's yurt to find her man. But what will become of the lama, especially a lama not yet acknowledged?

As she stares a familiar phrase—more question than answer—scarcely audible—is half-formed on her waiting lips,

"The lama knows: only the lama knows."

Later in the dark hours when talk comes easily she asks a question and gets a half-smothered answer.

"To keep all the rules is merely a monk's part. Only a lama can change them and remain something. Because of this night and the other nights which will follow men will believe me. I am a lama."

In that moment she, too, believes in him as never before, and as one would say a creed she murmurs,

"The lama knows."

VIII

Aluk Shiang Cheung sits on his great gray horse and rides swiftly along the trail, yet differently from those other times when he rode that same horse alone and free; going to council gatherings or secret trysts. Now he rides—a captive. His feet are tied to the stirrups, the ropes drawn under the horse's stomach from one to the other. The cuffs of his sleeves are strapped together tightly in front of him, his hands within—warm, it is true, but effectively tied. And the gray follows the pull, not of the reins, for they are knotted loosely on his neck, but of the lead rope which is held by a horseman who rides ahead. Around the prisoner armed riders move along the trail in a fairly compact group though their scouts are far ahead, far behind, and following the skyline on both sides of the valley through which they travel.

They come to the head of the valley and with redoubled precautions they climb the pass. Another section of the grasslands is spread before them as they come over the skyline: the ridges and hollows sharply marked in a pattern of sunshine that reddens and seems to turn faintly purple, and shadows that grow ever longer and blacker, for the sun is low in the west. Just beyond the edge of the pass and below the skyline the horsemen stop for a moment to search the landscape before them for sign of riders, other than themselves, abroad in the stretch of untouched grazing country between the land of the Black Tents and the region of the Southern Plain. They see nothing, and one of their scouts, suddenly outlined on the shoulder of a hill some distance beyond, signals for them to move on down into the deepening shadow.

Those shadows, which tell that night is already upon them, and that signal have their effect upon the horsemen. A certain tenseness in action and speech seems to leave and they talk among themselves with something like the beginning of ease. Some of their talk is directed toward the captive who rides in their midst; not all of it is even abusive but he gives no answer to any of it. With the crossing of the watershed the chances of possible pursuit and fighting—or at least a skirmish—are left behind, and the night which is just ahead promises almost complete protection. They can well begin to congratulate themselves: the Gurdu steward the most loudly of all as he keeps his big black horse close to the Lama's gray and taunts him briefly now and again. But still the lama does not speak.

With the crossing of the col the last chance of rescue is past. Through the blackness of a night which seems to rush upon them against the retreating sunshine, he rides into the land of his foes. That darkness is friendly to them and hides them but he well knows it cannot aid him to escape. Of what use are words?

He has not spoken since the first rush of armed men to his breakfast campfire caught him utterly off guard—rifle placed just out of reach to make more room around the fire and food. He attempted no defense or resistance for it was hopeless and useless, and his men, following his lead, also saved their lives: all but the one who as an acolyte had first joined himself to the fortunes of the One Who Had Come.

Because of that one hopeless move—dragging at a Mauser pistol that seemed to be caught in the case against his frantic slowness—he now lies face downward where he spun into the scattering fire as he fell, unless indeed the vultures have already come. The others were disarmed, deprived of their horses and set free. No one wants them as the managers of the Gurdu Great House want Aluk Shiang Cheung. No one waits for them as the monks of Gurdu wait in Tahk Thzang Lhamo for the coming of the pretender.

The managers of the Gurdu Great House and the monks of Gurdu have need of Aluk Shiang Cheung with a need that has been growing for three years. It has been growing ever since the night when Aluk Shiang Cheung—the pretender, the steward calls him as he guides his horse close in the dark and tries to sting him into speech with all the taunts his mind and tongue can summon —kept Wan Chen Mtso in his yurt until after sunrise; keeping her there, too, in that light to serve and share his early tea.

He became the son-in-law of the great Rgyal-wo Wang—somewhat decadent scion of a long line of kings who once ruled all

Amdo—but a king nevertheless. He became son-in-law, for that night together in the white yurt of the lama was no passing affair. From that night on through the nights and the days Wan Chen Mtso was his wife. She served his early tea, she managed his herds, she entertained his guests, and always she was waiting at the door of the yurt when he returned from those long rides on which he traveled alone on his own mysterious concerns, or from the more routine journeys when he toured the land of the Black Tents, the Sokwo, and all the other regions where his fame as a lama was established. Always she stood at the door of the yurt: pride and passion in lifted head and long eyes, to welcome him home to his fireside and to possession of her.

From that first morning his affairs had prospered anew and differently than before. Wealth, prestige and success had already been his. He was a great magician; a learned monk. Even Gurdu was prepared to admit that. But no monk dared serve religion as he continued to serve after breaking a monkish vow. Wan Chen Mtso, king's daughter of famous beauty, waiting at the door of his yurt, was the astounding triumphant proof that he was no mere monk. He continued to be a great magician. Many professed themselves scandalized yet they sought the services and bought the prayers of one who was great enough to be above all rules. He must be a lama. To the name Aluk Shiang Cheung—a name already accepted far and wide—men here and there began in whispers to add a sub-title—the greatest of all—"Gurdu Savior."

This was not only in the region of the Black Tents where he had already been accepted to some degree. Even among the Twelve Tribes of the Southern Plain, in the regions where as yet he dare not go, and where men dare not mention his name, for the combined power of Ngawa, Thsa-ru-ma, and Gurdu effectively threatened death to anyone who made part with him, even there strange rumors began to circulate. Old stories heard and half-forgotten were retold.

Once in the great tent of the Soktsong chief, satellite of Ngawa though he was, the story was told of what a pilgrim had once said. At least some of it was told or retold. It had been first whispered for three pairs of ears only, but the wind had stolen bits of the story and mixed them strangely. That capricious wind had carried that mixture into the night and what the wind had carried was the garbled tale that was told. The chief of Soktsong had laughed but

had turned stern and deadly serious when someone volunteered
the additional information that Aluk Shiang Cheung rode one of
the prize grays of the Soktsong herd.

Sometime later the old horse herder of Gurdu went on pilgrimage to Kumbum but never came back to the Gurdu encampment. Yet a message came back to his friends saying that he had
found service with a lama that loved horses and knew how to ride.
But his friends dared not say where it was that he had found such
service.

Suddenly, too, Musa seemed to tire of his business and the
gathering of wealth in Lhamo, and went to Taochow Old City, on
the Chinese frontier, to live and trade. There he continued to treat
his Tibetan customers to drinks out of a brown jug. But tribesmen
who traded with him when they visited the Chinese city with the
annual trade caravan said that he himself had again taken to
drink, and when drunk told wild tales. Once Ah Ta, chief of Rzachdumba, visited and spent a night with him. But Ah Ta never said
anything to anyone though thereafter he also visited Aluk Kong
Thang, his brother in Labrang.

With the increasing possibility of acceptance as the Gurdu
Lama, Aluk Shiang Cheung seemed, however, himself to lose some
of the intensity of his purpose to win that recognition. The lama
who rode like a layman with a silver-trimmed Russian rifle on his
back and a gold-trimmed Lhasa sword in his girdle found life very
pleasant: most pleasant of all when the howling of the encampment
dogs followed him with a rush to the door of his yurt, and a figure
outlined for a moment against the light that poured through the
open doorway said,

"Ah, you have come. Well come—the lama knows—well
come."

And moved to his horse's head; holding it as she had once held
it on a hilltop to help a lama dismount at her fire and come into
her life.

Rather it was Wan Chen Mtso herself who held him to the
struggle. Life was very pleasant for her, too, but a strange desire
for power—the stronger for the very fact that her house was the
house of a somewhat decayed tradition of power—refused her
complete satisfaction even with the possession of Aluk Shiang
Cheung. She had won a golden god to her arms but she wanted
him to be even more of a god on a still higher plane. So she dream-

ed of the Gurdu Great House; daring fate to debar her from it if
Aluk Shiang Cheung won his place within.

All these things: rumors, stories, intrigues, threats, and the
menace of new combinations in the power politics of the tribes of
Amdo bothered the Gurdu Great House more and more. The
Sacred Ram in bewilderment learned to curse the pretender lama
—son-in-law of Rgyal-wo Wang—wondering all the while in his
heart of hearts who that disturbing figure really was, for he, the
Sacred Ram, was forced to attend innumerable sessions where all
that was discussed was how to get rid of the pretender—the false
one. The Gurdu Lama himself never worried. He never worried
about anything for life was always like a dream in which he was
well-fed and that was enough. But his two brothers, the two
ombos, fiercely jealous of newly gained power and sensitive to all
that threatened their interest, never ceased to search for a solution
—swift and final—of their sudden legacy of trouble. And the steward, his soul dark with a hate born of fear and its remembrance,
dreamed of Aluk Shiang Cheung—so even he called the One Who
Had Come—finally in his hands.

The solution that the most elaborate planning could not bring
came through a chance word spoken by a pilgrim as he ate in the
Gurdu Guest Hall and talked with his hosts. Because of that word
the Gurdu raiders have caught Aluk Shiang Cheung off guard by
his breakfast fire, and without loss to themselves have taken him
prisoner.

So he rides through a darkness that protects his enemies but
gives him no chance of escape. He is hungry and thirsty and his
great fox fur hat has come askew over one eye, but he cannot
straighten it and he speaks to no one. He has not spoken since
they rushed upon him and it was suddenly too late to use his
silver mounted rifle or even the Lhasa sword. They have taken
those from him.

Armed only with silence he rides through the dark; riding not
toward an open doorway flooded with light where a figure comes
to hold his horse's head, as a king's daughter once held it when
she lost a token which only love could regain, but riding toward
death that surely comes to meet him though it may be tardy with
agony's long delays. Yet he straightens in the saddle, shifting his
weight somewhat onto his feet bound though they are in the stirrups. At least he will ride toward that death as a true horseman

should ride and maybe it will not be too long in coming to meet him when the ride shall have ended.

"Your place is ready for you in the Gurdu Great House," taunts the steward speaking once and again.

But Aluk Shiang Cheung is armed with silence and does not answer.

IX

The pool of light from a single butter lamp spreads in the darkness and pushes back the shadows of the limit of the walls and ceiling of the little room. As the lamp shifts and turns three faces float uncertainly in that pool of light—drifting successively into momentary clearness and again lost in the gloom.

That of the Gurdu steward shows most clearly for he holds the lamp and whichever way he turns it his face is never far away. In that light his face is nevertheless dark with hate born of fear. But hate come of fear is no longer weakened or troubled by fear. Aluk Shiang Cheung is in his power so completely that he no longer fears him as the One Who Has Come. For ten days he has been coming, once every day, to reassure himself that it is really Aluk Shiang Cheung—the onetime shining Lama of the cave entrance—who is fettered in the darkest cell of the lamasery prison. This time too he stares to be sure, but with a grim finality of purpose in his look.

The second face, that of the Gurdu ombo, tells of a gloating triumph that can scarcely contain itself. Once and again he furtively licks his lips as though he tasted something good, and the corners of his mouth twitch with eagerness. Yet the arrogance of his look cannot hide a half-ashamed curiosity, for this is the first time he has ever seen Aluk Shiang Cheung the Pretender. But having seen, his face seems to harden with resolve and again he runs the tip of his tongue over his full lower lip.

The third face that floats in the pool of light made by the butter lamp shows nothing. The marks of hunger, abuse, and the unwashed filth of ten days of close captivity seem something hung in front of and not a part of the face; that in itself is unmarked and expressionless. It is more than a face in repose: it is a face completely and purposefully blank—so blank no one knows the purpose that hides behind each feature. Even the eyes, oddly unwinking in the unexpected light, are not eyes but curtains tightly drawn no matter how the face seems to advance and recede in the changing light.

Ten days and nights have passed since the Gurdu raiders returned to the brow of the hill across the valley from the Gurdu lamasery and awakened the monks and the people of the "edge"— those who live in the hamlets grouped around the trading post— with announcement of their success. In answer to the sound of their shooting and of their shouting that seemed like the echo of a wolf pack cry, torches flashed in the darkness and answering hails came from the huts that flank the trail. The night was filled with questionings: asking for details and full confirmation. By the time the horsemen, with the noise of a troop of cavalry, had splashed through the ford near the lamasery the people of Tahk Thzang Lhamo knew that the Pretender to the throne of the Gurdu Lama was being brought to Lhamo as a prisoner. All through the lamasery lanes rang the cry,

"He has been taken. He has been taken."

That cry was followed by the confused mutter in hundreds of throats of the words, "The lama knows—Om mani padme hum— the lama knows!" Whatever of satisfaction, wonder, perplexity, or even pity and regret those words might mean.

Not all the people of the edge, nor even all of the monks of the lamasery were glad: many of those who were loudest in their rejoicing had secret qualms, for tragedy was certainly near. Some still questioned, even when the chorus of denunciation and rejoicing was the very loudest.

To themselves others still dared to whisper,

"The Gurdu Lama—the real lama—is to be killed."

Then they waited till the dawn of the day should come, and with it the confirmation of their fears. In the minds of all there was uncertainty about one thing only: no one was sure just what kind of a death the Pretender would die, but that die he would no one doubted; himself the least of all.

Instead ten days passed. He himself did not know the exact length of that long wait. In the darkness, cold and numbing agony of his fetters he had no knowledge of the duration of time except as measured by the visits of one who at irregular intervals brought him food and drink in insufficient quantity. So also he had no idea whether it was day or night when the flickering light of the butter lamp showed him two faces instead of one, and he knew that his time was near: his time of contest or trial if not of death.

Through the curtain of eyes that showed nothing and told nothing he recalls the steward and then intuitively recognizes the ombo for what he is. Each face swims in the light like a portent. They are linked one to another with a common purpose yet each one is different in plan and intensity of purpose.

To that purpose the steward speaks to say something he said a score of times on the trail.

"Your place in the Gurdu Great House is ready for you."

But he knows the absurd futility of his taunt as soon as he has spoken and in that sense of frustration he cannot keep from speaking again.

"Mouth of hell, we'll make you speak. I'll..."

The eyes of the captive are quite blank: his spirit withdrawn to some far place. The steward brings the lamp still closer to his face and the light washes over the contours like the tide at flood flowing over a rock. The features change as the shadows shift and change, and on either side of the face the two ears—full lobed and unusually long as true lama's ears should be—are suddenly revealed in the lamp light. The monstrous outline of the head fills one corner and wall of the cell but the expression of the face does not change. There is no expression; only utter blankness. Against that blankness as though it were a personal insult and challenge before which he cannot contain himself the ombo hurls one word with all his might.

"Speak!"

The eyes do not change, but the shadows shift and dance over the face for the steward moves the lamp with a threatening gesture.

"Useless to tell him to speak. I tried for a day and a night but I was commissioned to bring him in unharmed. Now let me try something else. Mouth of hell, I'll make him talk."

The ombo again licks his lips. This time they are twitching nervously, but he motions the steward to silence.

"Speak and tell who you are, you who call yourself Aluk Shiang Cheung. Tell who you are and what your family, and we will return you to that family unharmed. But speak or we leave you no tongue with which ever to speak again."

The ombo's voice is hoarse with some strange excitement and his hand, which rests on the arm of the steward, is trembling to make the shadows dance fantastically on the wall and ceiling of the cell.

"Speak!"

His voice rises almost to a scream for against all reason and the evidence of his own ears he is tempted to believe that he has uttered no sound, for no word seems to reach the prisoner in that far place where he has taken refuge.

"I'll make him speak. Let me..."

The steward places his lamp on the floor and breaks off his sentence as he turns toward the ombo asking for a signal.

It comes, and a hurried question.

"Do we need to call anyone?"

"We are two and he is already fettered."

Fettered or not the prisoner makes no movement of either comprehension or resistance, and they tie him face downward to the floor; his arms spread wide with the wrists strapped to rings in the planking; his fettered feet bound down in the same way. The ombo does his part with nervous trembling hands, clearing his throat again and again but the steward ties the knots with hands that are steady and savage with purpose. He then turns down the prisoner's yellow cloak passing his hand up and down the hollow in the flesh that follows the length of the backbone.

"Yes, Aluk Shiang Cheung, your place is ready and we will make you talk as a lama should talk when he takes his place. You are cold now. We will give you heat soon. But maybe you would prefer to talk before I begin, you hell-bent one who dares to call yourself Aluk Shiang Cheung."

Actually the steward expects no answer and without a pause goes on with what he is set to do. From where he had placed it on entering the cell he picks up a strip of fine Chinese incense about two fingers wide and a foot long, and holds one end in the flame of the lamp until every tip is red. The flame of the lamp is bent and blackened by the incense stick and little gusts of smoke swirl upward. So shadows and hints of an angry red glow chase each other across the face of the captive as it rests on the floor only a foot or so distant from the lamp. Those shadows and angry glints are reflected in the eyes but otherwise there is no change in their expression even when the stick of incense is lifted and the yellow flame burns clear once more.

"Speak!"

The steward's words come through clenched teeth. The ombo too draws his breath with a sucking noise as though the corners of his mouth were wet. The incense stick is laid in the long hollow in the flesh, the red end just between the shoulder blades.

There is silence in the little room. The body of the prisoner rests as before; arms and feet strapped to the floor, face turned slightly sidewise and resting on the planks, the eyes fixed on the flame of the lamp. Not a flicker of an eyelash signals when the moments begin to spin to the lash of pain, but the eyes change. The pupils, already dilated by the darkness, open to the very border of the iris—black openings in which the light from the candle is reflected and then lost. The steward watching them with a practiced curious eye, poises his hand just over the prisoner's back ready to pick up the fragment of hell lying there and repeats the word,

"Speak!"

The moments spin on: lifetimes in the drawing of a breath and yet swift as the passage of light. A faintly bitter odor haunts the room and stings the nostrils of the steward with a memory out of a half-forgotten past. For an instant he can hear the roar of a great fire and see the gust of smoke that pours from that fire as the body of the Gurdu Lama was burned and the tribesmen of the Great Plain watched that burning. There is more than curiosity in his look as he peers at the wide open eyes of the captive, and with anticipation sharp as pain he waits for speech, for again he has begun to know fear as he knew it at the mouth of the Drag Kar cave.

"Om mani padme hum!" gasps the ombo. "He is not a man— the lama knows—not a man. He is . . ."

He bites off the words with a sucking intake of breath and backs away from the face before him. The steward's face turns darker than ever with the shadow of the resurrected fear. Yet maybe that potent red glow halfway down the back of the one so completely in his power has ceased to burn. Maybe magic has caused it to die out. If so all is explained. He shifts his position to see and so maybe reassure himself, but instead stares like one bewitched at a red coal in the blackest hollow of the shadow that hides the prisoner's back: a fiery jagged spot that neither moves nor is entirely stationary. With a sudden sense of futility he realizes that, bound though he may be, the prisoner after all is not completely in his power; perhaps will never be completely in his power. At least he knows the prisoner will never speak though the red coal moves slowly through the shadows to the very end.

The incense stick burns on and the faintly bitter odor comes more strongly to the nostrils of those who watch.

"Not a man—not a man—maybe he is..."

The ombo has backed against the wall and babbles wildly in half-finished sentences. Then the steward moves his arm and picks up the half-consumed incense stick, saying in a grim, cold voice:

"No use that we wait for this to burn to the end. He will not speak."

Yet before he picks up the lamp he bends close to look at the face of the man on the floor. Obeying his beckoning hand, the ombo moves away from the wall to join him and together they stare at a face that is still a face of compelling beauty. In that face two eyes—black as no ordinary eyes ever can be, for the pupils hide all the iris—look back at them. The once drawn curtains are wide open. The mouth, the brows, the whole face is alive with an emotion that vibrates like a living thing that springs through the eyes like a wild beast, and the ombo and steward know that they now are hated as they have never been hated before. Grudgingly the steward speaks.

"Looks like a lama. By the Presence he certainly does."

It is true. Every other detail is lost in the shadows. Only the face—a face like the face of Buddha on the idol scrolls—swims in the light and the two long, heavily lobed ears of a true lama complete the resemblance.

"What ears! But we will yet make him hear if we can't make him speak just now."

The steward is again poised and calculating. Somehow out of this persistent silence maybe he can make a trap for the lama-like one. It no longer makes any difference to him whether the prisoner is the lama or not. Equally in either case he must die.

"Lama ears though they are he will have to hear and die."

The words spur the ombo to sudden unexpected action. Those ears more than anything else threaten him and his position. The one who will not speak carries the visible claim to all he does not say on both sides of his face. Lama ears! There is the glint of a blade in the uncertain light and where one ear was there is an odd irregular pattern in red. Before the steward can interfere, even if he is so minded, the knife flashes again. The eyes do not change though now they stare out of a strange mutilation and the face is framed as by a red scarf wound in a strange irregular pattern that ends in a dark pool on the floor. The face is no longer the face of the one who might be the Gurdu Lama. Its onetime beauty is a grotesque mockery but the eyes are still unwinking and under that strange regard the steward is in haste to be gone, and fumbles at the door lock with his hands behind his back. He is oddly reluctant to turn his back to the prisoner but, holding the light between, keeps his face toward the one on the floor.

"The Earless One—the Earless One."

The steward mutters the words as though they were the words of an incantation and speaks earnestly to the ombo. But the ombo shudders suddenly to find an ear—long and full lobed—still tightly clenched in his left hand.

The Lamalike One was once armed with silence but for the Earless One maybe that silence is a weapon that can be turned against him. The steward has already begun to forge that weapon as he and the shuddering ombo leave the cell.

X

The ombo brings his long speech to an end. He has heaped denunciation and condemnation on Aluk Shiang Cheung and piled arguments upon proof to show that for the crimes of sacrilege and impiety he is worthy only of death. At the end the ombo turns from the great gathering in the courtyard and galleries of the Gurdu Great House and addresses one short sentence to the accused. Yet as he speaks he is sure that the prisoner will not answer. He speaks the words nevertheless, for they are a part of the trap that is to be made of silence.

"Gurdu Lama—yes or no. Speak!"

The courtyard is filled with chiefs and headmen from the twelve tribes of the Great Southern Plain, from the five tribes of the upper Tebbu, from the tribes of the Thsa-ru-ma confederacy together with the leaders of the Ngawa principality headed by their young king. Rank on rank they fill the courtyard and overflow onto the porches that overlook the scene.

Only the men of Rzachdumba are missing—officially at least. Neither chief nor headmen are in their places. No one is sure about Rzachdumba. The very same night that Aluk Shiang Cheung was brought to Lhamo the night riders of Ah Ta the bold sounded an alarm in every encampment of his tribe. But the signal for which they were to wait—news of the death of the captive— never came. Not all the members of the crowd packed into dark doorways and corners of the porches around the courtyard are easily identifiable, and some whisper to one another that men of Rzachdumba are also present, though no one can specify just where they are.

The rumor is also current that the troops of the tribe are gathered behind the first ridge that forms the threshold to Tahk Thzang Lhamo—Goddess of the Tiger's Den. But that, too, is a rumor not verified and no one actually expects an attack. Still it might come. At least that much of uncertainty hangs over the gathering.

Such rumors mean little to the seven hundred and more men who have been gathered to pass sentence on Aluk Shiang Cheung. They represent the greatest aggregation of power and military might in all Amdo and whatever gestures Ah Ta the bold may choose to make count for but little with them. They have come to see for themselves how the impostor should die. It is a forgone conclusion that he is an impostor and that he should die. They are not gathered to give a verdict but to impose a sentence.

Yet a question stirs uneasily in the minds of many: the same question that has been whispered during the past month by those who live in Tahk Thzang Lhamo or who pass through on trading trips or forays. Why is the Pretender—Aluk Shiang Cheung—still alive? Why was he not killed that first night upon his arrival? And how is it that after torture and the loss of his ears, he has not conveniently died in the fifteen days it has taken to gather the notables of Amdo together! With a little carelessness—a slight forgetfulness about food or the releasing him from the floor so he could draw his cloak about him—it could have been arranged so easily. Yet he is alive. Chained to the post in the center of the courtyard but free to sit or stand and for all of his fetters he sits as a lama should sit: as the Enlightened One sits in the realm of bliss: as a golden one once sat in the sunlight at the mouth of a cave.

He now sits in a sunlight that gilds him with no glory to help out his dress or pose, but which reveals with pitiless clarity tatters, stains, filth and disfigurement. The yellow robe is nothing but a rag streaked with bloodstains and filth. His face is plastered with the record of twenty-five unwashed days and nights of close captivity, and a strip of dirty cloth is tied down over the sides of his head and under his chin. That crude bandage is stiff with dried blood and yellow with pus stains, and its presence has changed the very contours of the head; making it appear deformed and twisted. And though that misshapen head is held high, the shoulders of the captive are hunched as though he sought to lift the weight of his cloak from off his back.

Against the sun his eyelids are half-closed, for even the length of the ombo's speech hasn't given enough time for the eyes to

become accustomed to the day after the darkness of a night a
month long. They still appear unusually dark as they turn steadily,
taking in that section of the crowd that is grouped in front of him,
for the pupils are abnormally large and no one can tell what color
the eyes might once have been.

At the sudden end of the ombo's speech and with the sharp
command to speak the prisoner turns his head so as to take in, in
that steady searching regard, all of the crowd bit by bit, for directly behind the post to which he is chained there is only a blank
wall. Is he searching for some face or for some sign? His gaze
rests for seconds first here and then there, but the expression of
the face does not change. Before he ever looked he must have
known that all who are gathered there are enemies.

The ombos and the steward consult among themselves: his
deadly foes getting ready for the kill. The Sacred Ram stares with
aged eyes —yet eyes not too old to show hate and wish death for
him. The section where the Tebbus sit seems to rustle with a deep
sullen muttering. They are the ones who the night before sur-
rounded the Gurdu Great House gate, demanding that the impostor be brought out and delivered to them that they might cut him
in pieces and so avenge the insult to the Gurdu Lama—their only
Savior.

Stern and inscrutable, the Sohk-tsong chief bends his brow in
a fixed frown but one of the men in his party, who sits beside him,
moves uneasily in his place as the prisoner's eyes pass slowly over
him. The chief from Thsa-ru-ma, too, mutters imprecations deep
in his throat and keeps his hand upon his sword handle. There are
those in his retinue who watch him as though waiting for a signal
and it is rumored that the men of Thsa-ru-ma intend to take matters into their own hands by sudden violent action. Of the notables, only the young king of Ngawa seems like a detached
spectator, watching all that goes on with thoughtful, slightly quiz-
zical eyes that miss nothing.

Aside from these, the men of Ka-chu-ka, Shami, and a half-
score of other places stand close-pressed—rank on rank—staring
in an all but unanimous enmity at the one chained to the post. But
still there are those who are merely curious; waiting and watching
for anything to happen but having no wish one way or another.
And maybe there are others—one or two here and there—that
hope for some reprieve for the one already condemned: for some

sudden accident of mercy to divert punishment. Yet that thought is like the futile wish that lingers on the tomb of a hope already dead.

From faces that show or reflect only one feeling or at least give no encouragement, the captive's eyes are raised to take in the gray roofs of the Great House, some parts of which seem drunken with age and decay. Beyond the rooftops there is a sky that is doubly blue because of the threat of clouds that are massing in the distance. And in that blue sky the highest peak of the Iron Mountain God seems to peer over those gray rooftops to see what is taking place. So the chained one looks to see what sky and mountain have to tell him after twenty-five days of darkness.

His eyes have changed in the time he has been looking for whatever he expects or hopes to find in the crowd or the sky above. Certainly they are lighter in color and for some of the spectators that simple fact calls up ghosts. Maybe the steward, too, really sees those eyes for the first time when they pass slowly over him with a glance that is strange as things once known. It is time to make an end. Anyway the Tebbus are stirring and maybe the Thsaru-ma chief already thinks that the time of waiting is too long. The steward's elbow touches that of the ombo and on the contact the ombo speaks one sharp word.

"Speak!"

Yet he is completely certain that the chained one will not speak.

On that word, as answering a signal but not obeying a command, without a moment's pause or the half-audible hesitation that helps to clear the throat, Aluk Shiang Cheung speaks; the deep clear tones of his voice reaching to the farthest corner of the courtyard.

XI

"Who says that I, Aluk Shiang Cheung; living in the land of the Black Tents, son-in-law of Rgyal-wo Wang, am Aluk Shiang Cheung the Gurdu Lama? Could there not be two Shiang Cheungs —aluk or otherwise? You can easily know who I am. Ask the family of Wan-dro in the Ong-kor encampment of the Golok tribe of Gsar-ta—Gsar-ta which is farthest of all Golok tribes. Even though they do live far away ask them for the name of their third son. They can tell the story of his life until his twentieth year."

The Silent One has spoken. That astonishing fact itself loses, however, all importance compared to the significance of what he has said. To all intents he has said he is not the Gurdu Lama. What blows, threats and torture could not bring him to say has been uttered. The trial is ended. Or is it begun? With only a slight pause as if for breath, or to let amazement ring a bell in everyone's mind, he goes on. Yet as he continues to speak his voice and words undergo a subtle change.

"Twenty-six years ago I went on a pilgrimage. Twenty-six years ago when fall had begun and snow was in the air: twenty-six years ago when I was just beginning to be a man at the age of nineteen years: twenty-six years ago when a great need and a great danger sent me on pilgrimage to Lhasa the place of gods."

Twenty-six years! At each repetition of the words the men of the crowd, from the Ngawa king down to the commonest spectator hidden in the dark corners of the porches do sums in their minds or even click the beads of their rosaries to help their arithmetic, for it was twenty-six years ago that the Gurdu Lama disappeared from the Gurdu encampment and rode his horse to the river's bank on a morning when fall was beginning and snow was in the air. Yes, it was twenty-six years ago when the Gurdu Lama of sainted memory was just beginning to be a man at the age of nineteen years.

74

His manner of speaking changes with utterance of the next sentence spoken with the exaggerated consonants and long drawled vowels characteristic of the distinctive and famous dialect of Ngura. He might easily be a brave from Ngura talking, as he goes on with the tale.

"In the land of Ngura I began my pilgrim journey. In the land of Ngura where the great meadow plain borders Chiao-ko Warma just above the great whirlpool of Peacock Waters, just where the tents of the tribe are pitched when the fall haying is done, there in the land of Ngura I made the start of the long journey. There I started horseless and afoot as a beggar pilgrim to fulfill my vow. Yet the men of Ngura, though hostile to the men of the Twelve Tribes this side of Peacock Waters, are a generous folk, and were happy to help a poor pilgrim go the long trail to Lhasa the place of gods."

The two ombos, the Gurdu steward, the unruly lowering Tebbus, even the Sacred Ram who seldom has an idea of any kind, have all only one thought, as clear as though it had been chanted in chorus by every one. Ngura—the hostile land of Ngura—was the opposite bank of the place where the Gurdu Lama's horse had entered the river. In Ngura, too, then the pilgrimage began.

The prisoner again pauses and his eyes pass reflectively over the crowd. All shifting, every movement of any kind, has ceased. They still think of Ngura but the next words of his speech are no longer in that dialect. As completely as one changes from a garment of one color to that of another color, so his words are said as the Goloks say them. The differences between the vowels are exaggerated and unpronounceable prefixes are sounded as he talks of the life in the Black Nests in the speech of the Black Nest people.

"But for a beggar with a pack upon his back the pilgrim trail to Lhasa is long, and well it is that the Golok tribes are camped along some of the way—Archong, Gon-mong, Bu-wha-thsang, Lu-di-thsang, Kangghan, Kang-gsar, Gsar-ta—all of the tribes of the Black Nest peoples. Each one is a place where a pilgrim may rest, or wait for companions, or gain strength and provisions, or simply wait until the holy horoscopes tell that the way ahead is clear of evil influence. It is the land, Oh you people of the Great Southern Plain, of mountains and deep valleys and the everlasting house of snow of Amne Machen, the great snow peak. It is the land of the wild yak and the great wild sheep; the land of glaciers that fill the valley heads and of everlasting snows that block the passes. Yet there a pilgrim may live for months among the round heads; the people of the Black Nests; those who eat only meat and drink blood drawn from living cattle.

"Beyond the land of the Goloks, the high empty plain of the wilderness—empty of human life or the sight of cattle or herds— stretches toward a white wall of snow against the far blue sky. One marches and the legs grow weak and the appetite fails. The feet swell for the poison gas sickness of the Dang La pass has struck. Yet, however sick one may be, the world is empty except for the prayer 'Om mani padme hum!' carved on every rock and cliff: empty except for the footprints of those who have gone before and the bones of those who failed in their going. There my companions had to leave me to die. But I did not die, I could not die for I must get to the holy place of Lhasa and the meeting of my destiny."

By this time the attention, even sympathy, of the great crowd are utterly with the speaker. They, too, are going step by step toward the place of gods carried by the words of some wild Golok— uncut hair hanging to his shoulders—who leads the way for all: some wild Golok summoned into existence by the harsh sound of impossible consonant combinations and exaggerated vowels in the mouth of the prisoner. Abruptly he changes again to the strangest dialect the tribesmen of the Great Plain have ever heard: the sing- song mincing language of the Bodpa and the people of Lhasa itself.

"From Nagchuka onward I was in the land of the Bodpa: the land of villages, fields, and thousands of beggar pilgrims. There was truly little to eat as we tramped slowly onward toward Lhasa. The Bodpa think only of trade but we were only poor pilgrims seeking out of piety for merit in a sight of the Potala, seeking a chance to worship at the shrines of the holy place. But after days of wandering past the closed doors and sly contempt of the Bodpa we came to Lhasa and I to my destiny—the destiny that has made me a gift of the Sacred Magic and a wearer of the Yellow Cap."

He is a prisoner clad in rags and filth; chained and helpless. Instead of a cap of any sort he wears a foul bandage that covers a putrifying mutilation. Yet not one of all the crowd thinks of that contrast. They are hearing a tale that has made them forget for the moment their prejudices and bias. The tale is now told in a language they can understand but imperfectly yet the strange phrasing but adds fascination to what is told. It is the tale of a pilgrim monk who not only reached Lhasa but went on to Shigatze, crossed the frontier into India at Dorjeling, saw Benares, and Galicuta, and wandered far. Yet his wanderings ended. He holds his hearers in a sort of enchantment as he talks of scenes and places, but the journeying ceases—for a time at least in Lhasa again.

"I was a poor pilgrim monk and as such my destiny found me as I begged from door to door in the streets of Lhasa. I was taken into a lamasery as a tea boy to pour tea. Instead of pouring tea I learned to chant all the Sacred Writings. There I learned the mysteries of the doctrine: the perfection of the Eightfold Way. There I learned the Advanced Wisdom and the overcoming of ignorance. And as I learned the doctrine, so I learned the secrets of meditation and the Sacred Magic. Little by little power came to me until the chains of matter could no longer bind me. So I came to sit in air needing no support whenever I meditated fully. There I conquered distance and learned to see things happening as far away as ten days' ride on horseback because I could go there through the air on a spirit horse. There I learned to meditate and hold my breath until my soul turned inward and I was enlightened. In that enlightenment which came to me it was revealed I was a lama. So also the leaders of the lamasery were enlightened and all knew that I was a lama. This is all that came to me when my destiny found me in the Sera lamasery of Lhasa."

Again the prisoner stops and his gaze wanders over the crowd. Does he see a slight movement around the Sohk-tsong chief as though a gust of wind no one else can feel has set their heads to moving with a faint whispering like the rustling of leaves? The name of the Sera lamasery blew out of a starless night as part of a tale the wind had born. How blows it now?

Far in another corner of the courtyard someone else—a monk in tattered garments—with a quick movement throws his mantle over his head to hide his face, for he had once been a pilgrim to Lhasa and had visited the Sera lamasery. Maybe the prisoner sees such movement, maybe not. But more than ever before his face tells nothing, and his eyes have ceased to ask questions. He only looks to see what next to tell and having seen goes on with his tale.

"I was a lama but no one knew what lama, so I set myself to find out. I went to Nam Mtso the sacred lake and lived on the island that floats like a raft. There I learned the riddle of the future for in the wisdom of that enlightenment difference of time does not exist. I could read the future clearly without confusion. But I could not find out what lama I was. Then I went to the gorges of the Tsang-po where the serpent spirits swarm, and living there in seclusion, I learned the reason and source of disease and so its cure. But I could not find out what lama I was. Then I lived in a cave on the highest mountains, close to Kang-chen-junga: lived in a cave among the snows like Milaraspa the singer of the Hundred Thousand Songs. And like him I had only cotton robes but the heat of tumo filled my body so the snows were melted a fathom from where I sat. But I could not find out what lama I was.

"Armed with power, I left the place of gods and all those farther places where wisdom is perfected in those who conquer ignorance and meditate aright, and came back to the land of Amdo. I left the Bodpas in their forts and villages. I left the Potala where the great holy Lama sits—with reverence—and came back to the Black Tents, for I was a lama yet seeking to know what lama I was."

Like the shoutings that come through the night, shoutings blurred by wind and tempestuous rain, the last part of his tale has been told in language hard to understand. Suddenly like a whisper spoken on a still night by one who sits by the same fire, his speech is once more clear; slightly blurred by the niceties of the Labrang pronunciation yet having too the tricks and mannerisms of the speech of the Twelve Tribes of the Southern Plain.

"I am a lama and for that my ears have been cut from my head. Ask to know if they were not lama's ears. And now that they have been taken, take the rest; my lips, my nose, my eyes, my hands, my feet, and whatever else is left. Yet when all is taken I shall still be a lama seeking to know what lama I am. In each re-incarnation I shall come; still seeking to know. Tell me, you who are gathered here, what lama am I? My words are ended."

Amidst all the confusion of baffled hate and real bewilderment that one question rides triumphant in each man's thoughts. Even the surly Tebbus are silent in the silence of the speaker. They too would like to know what lama he is. His friends—or converts—

are already muttering the answer to their neighbors, but there can be no final answer for a month, now there is only a long murmur throughout the crowd—the lisping of the wind.

"The lama knows—only the lama knows."

It will take a month for messengers on fast horses to make the round trip to and from the Ong-kor encampment among the Gsarta Goloks. For a month at least the prisoner will wait: his enemies too will wait for nothing can be done until the messengers come back. But he seems to be waiting now for an answer to come from somewhere beyond the crowd in the courtyard, for he is looking only at the peak of the Iron Mountain God poised in the blue sky.

The glare of the sun has done its work. His eyes are oddly light in color.

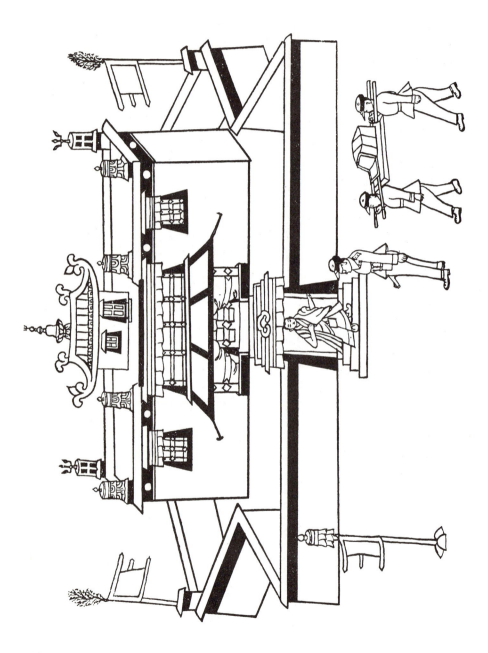

XII

The Iron Mountain God, high in a sky where shreds of mist trail from the peak; the weathered roofs and staggering gate drunken with decay, of the Gurdu Great House; the grim red walls of the great enclosure, together with the monks that crowd every point of vantage look down on the strangest sight ever seen in Tahk Thzang Lhamo. The Chinese general Li Wen Whua, Defense Commissioner of The Border, on a tour of inspection where never a Chinese general was seen before, signals his bearers to stop, and his light mountain chair comes to a halt in front of the Gurdu Great House gate.

The bearers steady the poles at half height and the general slips out of the chair. His staff of seven or eight officers and aides climb down from their mounts with considerable difficulty, and with no unanimous or certain preference for the right or left side of the horse. The bodyguard of not more than a dozen foot soldiers, indifferently armed with very inferior rifles, comes to attention, and the stage is set for a somewhat dried up little man—gray and not very impressive—who for all of the black cape he wears, shivers slightly as the wind seems to drop from the peak of the Iron Mountain God with added sharpness.

He stares with a pensive, non-committal air at the gate of the Gurdu Great House—a gate half-open—and in the gateway one lone monk, muffled in his mantle, stares back with an odd assumption of indifference. Above the gateway there is a tablet with gilt lettering announcing that this is the "House of Western Peace and The Perfect Law." It bears the seal of the emperor T'ung Chih who reigned over sixty years ago. The lettering is somewhat battered and weathered but a still more timeworn inscription hangs beside it—a tablet over a hundred years old—that compliments the "Living Buddha of Ten Thousand Perfections."

The emperors of the past thus signified their regard for the

81

Gurdu Great House. The general reads the inscriptions with an oddly pedantic air, appearing more and more inoffensive and even futile. The crowd of monks who are gathering begin to titter slyly. "Perfect Law" and "Ten Thousand Perfections", so Chinese sovereignty in the past spoke of the Gurdu Great House. Suddenly, sharply, and with no preamble, the representative of the Chinese government of today speaks.

"I am the superior representative of the government. I am making an official visit. Tell the rulers who live in this house to come out and meet me. I have orders to give to them, my subordinates."

The order is repeated a second time in Tibetan as the interpreter does his part.

Without giving either bow or acknowledgment the monk in the doorway disappears. For a moment the general speaks to his staff of the calligraphy of the past century, discoursing of its beauty, and then falls silent, drawing his cape closer as he waits. The crowd of monks has grown to suggestive and significant pro-portions, but the General does not see them; he only waits.

An inter-tribal war, that boiled over the Chinese frontier in acts of lawlessness and a number of robberies, resulted in the entrance of Chinese troops into Amdo to effect a settlement. At the head was the Commissioner of Border Defense himself, charged not only with the task of settling the dispute, but commissioned to make a tour of inspection as far as Lhamo, the Southern Plain, and the upper Tebbu. Partly by using Tibetans already under Chinese control and obedient to Chinese orders, partly by a show of military force, and partly by sheer bluff—for Chinese infantry are not the best troops for action against the horsemen of Amdo—the General and his party have arrived at Lhamo.

The entire force has been quartered in the rival lamasery of Sechu across the stream from the Gurdu lamasery and the Tibetans of the region, constitutionally predisposed to view them with hatred and dislike, are at a loss as to how to treat them. Their numbers are insignificant. Within two days and nights ten times that number of hard-riding warriors could be raised from among the Twelve Tribes. Yet they are in Lhamo in all seeming confidence; commanding service from everyone, as is the habit of the military the world over.

Nor is their armament impressive. Their rifles are second-rate, the few horses they have are jaded and in poor condition, and the men who handle and ride them do so in a manner that makes the Tibetans roar with laughter. As a military force the Chinese column is not impressive in the eyes of the horse-wise and gun-wise Tibetans and yet the officers of that column seem so sure. Maybe that is because the wires of a radio receiving and sending set have been set up, and the rumor circulates that the General has talked with his headquarters in China and that bombing planes are ready to come to his aid if necessary.

The crowd that has gathered while the general waits outside the Gurdu Great House gate knows all these things and more, and the members of that crowd are well-tempted to amusement at the expense of the tired looking little man who stands there and waits; reading memorial tablets the while.

They do not know that he was once a teacher in the Whampo Military Academy and that at one time he had Chiang Kai Shek in his classes, that he was an officer in the Northern Punitive Expedition and helped take Nanking, that he commanded troops in the fighting in Shanghai, and that he has been through bombing, heavy artillery barrages and scenes of such fighting as the tribesmen of Amdo have no experience of. There are many things the crowd do not know and yet because they sense their own ignorance and have vague misgivings they forebear to laugh aloud—as yet. They will laugh later when the Gurdu Great House gate swings to and the odd little Chinaman has to turn and go away. Laugh: yet maybe break into action with stones or even more warlike weapons. For the moment, like the General, they await the return of the messenger.

He comes and there is a trace of bewilderment mixed with an insolence of word and manner that has its source elsewhere than in his own thought and decision. He too, is surprised that he has not been ordered to close the gate on the hated strangers. Instead, he delivers his message in a voice calculated to reach the ears of the crowd, whether the little man in the black cape understands it or not.

"The ombos and the steward are all busy: too busy to see anyone now. But if the stranger wants to wait he can wait in the Gurdu Great House guestroom."

The crowd understands. When the little man enters the gate

to take his place in the Great House guestroom it will be time to laugh, and if he turns and leaves—getting into the sedan chair to be borne on the shoulders of men back to the place where he is staying—then it will also be time to laugh and maybe even think of stones or weapons. But the messenger does not understand: he is still puzzled because he was not told to shut the gate in the face of the stranger.

The interpreter changes the clipped burred Tibetan syllables into sing-song Chinese and the General understands: understands maybe better than all of them, for his interest in calligraphy vanishes.

"Guard, stand to arms to guard this gateway with rifles cocked. Let no one come in. Officers, do your duty for our common country and leader. This is war. Follow me. Interpreter, tell this man he dies unless he does exactly as I say."

They are all—even the General—armed with overgrown Mauser automatics and they do the one thing no one expected. They charge into the Gurdu Great House with guns in their hands. A gasp of amazement is the only immediate reaction of the crowd and then it is too late to do anything. The General and his staff have disappeared within and the riflemen standing at the gate are nothing more than pawns. The real game is being played within. As they listen for the sound of shooting no one thinks any more of laughter.

The messenger is an unwilling guide but with the muzzle of a gun pressing between his shoulderblades he can be nothing else and he guides the General and his staff—not to the Great House guestroom—but to the private room of the Gurdu Lama himself. The two ombos are there, the Sacred Ram is there, the steward is there. They are all there: just beginning to have a good laugh at the poor little man in the black cape who waits outside the Gurdu Great House gate, and they are also just about to send orders for the troops of the Twelve Tribes to gather.

As he enters the room the General sees none of them. He sees only the lama robed and splendid; appearing on his throne like the only source of all power and rule. Assuredly this is the ruler who was told to meet him outside the gate; the one who sent calculated impertinence instead. Before the startled Tibetans realize what is taking place the General has the Lama by the collar and has dragged him from his throne. As he stumbles and sprawls from his

pedestal to a heap on the floor the General menaces him with his
pistol and says briefly,

"Take him out and shoot him."

The lama has lived for nineteen years in the Gurdu Great
House as a god lives throughout unbroken cycles in the western
heaven. In all that time he has only learned how to receive worship and bestow blessing. For that his seat has been soft and he has
eaten the fat and the sweet; leaving responsibility to others. He
has heard of war, he has blessed the councils of arbitration when
peace is made—sitting aloof like a golden god—and he has even
taken a childish pleasure in the weapons his guard of honor carried when some chief has received him in state, but for all of that he
has lived in a vacuum, no matter how closely the great winds of
the tempestuous power politics of Amdo have blown over his
head. Yet he does not need the stammered interpretation in Tibetan of the General's order to tell him that he is now in harsh contact with life—maybe with death. He is neither receiving worship
nor bestowing blessing and he knows it. With that knowledge in-
stinctively and surprisingly he reverses his role.

"With reverence—with reverence."

It is a prayer he is saying as he knocks his head on the floor
and grovels at the feet of the little gray man in the black cape. The
General's accusing menacing pistol discovers the others and his
order is repeated, yet with a somewhat different wording.

"Take them out and shoot them—this one repents."

There is only one thing to do. Given an equal chance, the
ombo's arrogance, the steward's grim stubbornness, and the stiff-
ness of the Sacred Ram's aged joints might keep them one and all
unbending in the face of danger. Given an equal chance, they can
outface maybe even General Li Wen Whua. But they don't have
an equal chance for their lama is already down on the floor. He is
a tool, a brother, or a child to one or another of them and yet
even for them he is the Lama—the Presence to be worshiped even
as they demand that others worship him. And he is on the floor
abjectly bumping his head to the "wretched Chinaman." There is
only one thing to do. They too repent and bow to save their lives,
and while all five are bowed to the floor the General gives them a
lecture on political economy and statecraft, with excursions into
the realm of international law.

"With reverence—with reverence—."

It is all they can say in answer to what they hear—most of which they cannot understand even with the interpreter's best endeavors. But General Li Wen Whua is not only a professor of political science; he is also the very hard-headed leader of an expeditionary forces needing supplies, transportation and service. He orders supplies and corvees of transport. He orders forage and fuel and an escort of Gurdu riders as far as the land of the upper Tebbu and to each order the five—lama, ombos, steward and poor old Sacred Ram—bump their heads on the floor and say,

"With reverence—with reverence.—"

All possible exactions have been made and even fines levied. The General is out of breath but his erstwhile enforced study of calligraphy, while the impertinent wind whipped the skirts of his black cape, still rankles. So he searches in his mind for one thing more of command and enforced obedience with which to lash the rebels. He remembers a tale recently heard and but half believed.

"You have a prisoner whose ears you cut off: a thing entirely contrary to civilized law and principles. You have such an one?"

"With reverence—yes—with reverence."

"Nothing more is to be done to him. If he dies I will hold you responsible."

"But your Excellency should know that the prisoner is a poor thievish vagabond. Like a masterless dog he has no one behind him; he has no patron and no right."

The first ombo, stung to the quick, has spoken before the unfamiliar restraining effect of fear can stop his tongue. The Earless One and his fate have nothing to do with this officious stranger. And by what mischance has the Chinese learned of his existence?

"Ah, you are still rebellious, are you? Bind his hands and we take him with us as a hostage until we reach the upper Tebbu. You poor ignorant Tibetan, do you not know that the poorest beggar has a protector and everyone has his rights as a man? The government of China is the protector of everyone and of this one in particular. If I hear that harm has come to him after I leave this place the iron birds will come and your lamasery will be no more. It is time for us to go. You come with us. You others, the four of you, can stay."

There is no sign of laughter or thought of mirth in the crowd that watch the return of the Chinese general, who sits somewhat huddled up in his chair with the black cape wrapped around him, for the ombo walks beside the bearers; keeping step although his hands are tied behind his back.

In a dark cold cell a prisoner who knows nothing of these events finds that night that his evening meal is sufficient in quantity and quality for the first time, but he makes no comment to the jailor even when his fetters are lightened and an extra garment is given him. He only thinks that they wish to be sure to keep him alive until the messengers return. After that only his destiny knows what will happen. He, the Knowing One, does not know that the great Chinese government has been declared his protector. Maybe he will never know.

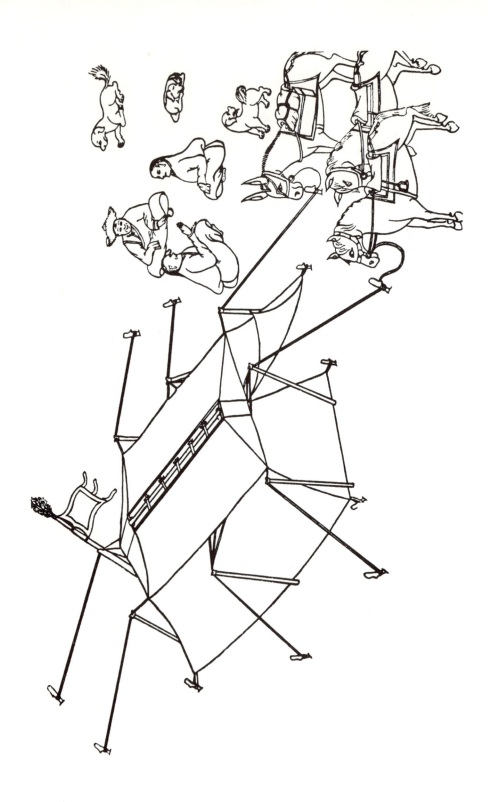

XIII

The famous great mastiffs of the Sohk-tsong chief turn back toward the rim of the encampment quite discouraged; equally by the threats of their master as by the stones hurled at them by his companion—his advisor and right-hand man. The third man who walks with them is the stranger the dogs sought to get at, but he is protected by the other two and already far enough away from the tents to be safe. His pack mules and horses are tied at the door of the chief's tent and his traveling companions are still eating and drinking inside. But he has news of private import to tell, for he is the Gurdu steward, and what he has to say is for the ears of the Sohk-tsong chief and his chief headman alone.

The three stop within full view of the encampment and take their seats at the edge of the bluff. There the sod ends abruptly and the sides of the bank fall steeply to the river below. From where they sit the entire ten-mile course of White Waters, to where it joins Peacock Waters, is visible—a long shining band between the russet meadows and flats of the Sohk-tsong fall pastures. At one point it broadens into the half-mile ford where at low water the caravans can cross by wading and so save the ferry crossing down at the mouth, where Sohk-tsong lamasery shows white and clear against the mountain that stubbornly bends the knee of Peacock Waters.

A gray snow-heavy sky hangs close over river and meadows, and the three men draw the collars of their furs tightly around their necks, for the wind, flattening the long grass, is sharp with the sting of a storm that is yet to come.

"It snows soon. Better wait and stay over. Besides, my son will be back tonight and can help you on your way tomorrow. Why be in such a hurry?"

The Sohk-tsong chief is being the hospitable host and yet also something more. He has known the Gurdu steward for years and knows that in his cautious, secretive way he needs all possible help to get something important finally told. Even with such a lead the steward still hesitates, his dark face blurred with indecision. But if he is to go on immediately he must tell at least something, and his mission is so urgent he dare not stay when the period of daylight left him in the afternoon will take him far.

"I must see the king of Ngawa as soon as possible, and if I go right on I may catch him as he visits the fall encampment. That will save at least two days. If we can only decide what should be done before everyone knows. If everyone should know and scold and blame that would be bad enough but what they may do—are almost certain to do—is laugh. Mouth of hell—when the tent people begin to laugh how can that laughter be stopped?"

The steward's somber regard probes at the faces of the chief and his man, as though he suspected them of being the first to laugh. Yet nothing can be farther from laughter than the stern set face of the chief, and as for the other it is so far hidden in his collar that it might as well not be a face at all.

"It isn't only the matter of the coming of the miserable Chinaman. You heard about that, didn't you?"

"What miserable Chinaman? Tell the account of it."

The Sohk-tsong chief's face is inscrutable. It tells nothing. If it is ever to break into laughter that laughter is still long in coming. But the face of his companion is out of hiding; hung above the collar of his coat like a question mark; waiting for the steward's answer.

"You heard about the Chinese officer, surely you heard? The Chinese officer that came to Lhamo leading some miserable soldiers? There weren't so many of them and their rifles were poor. Maybe if we had called out the troops of the Twelve Tribes immediately—but everyone was afraid because of the machine that talks through space. He came to see us—of the Gurdu Great House—and there was trouble. We should have either fought him or received him. We did neither and there was difficulty—some difficulty—."

"After he entered the Great House?"

The Sohk-tsong chief has not spoken. It is the other one who fires the question like the crack of a rifle on a still night, but the shadow of a frown passes over the chief's face and he interjects—smoothly but authoritatively—a question.

"You did not receive him then? But did he enter? We want to know."

The steward stares accusingly at the two but again their faces are completely blank. He takes up the tale where it was broken off.

"—difficulty and some trouble but the general—the Chinaman —was angry and he said that the Earless One must be spared all further injury of any sort: that we would be responsible. What should he care about the vagabond anyway? What a hell-bent Chinaman says means little enough. But he had the big ombo as a hostage for three days so we could do nothing, well though we wished to. And the Sacred Ram is an old fool—would not let me—."

The steward's voice falters and bogs down in conflicting emotions and reviving indecision. He suddenly is no longer sure of his hearers, for the things he wishes to say are completely dangerous: dangerous for the speaker and dangerous, too, for even the hearers.

"So you did not harm the Earless One after all? The Thsa-ru-ma chief said he would not live until the messengers got back. But after what the Chinese general said—you decided—it seemed—."

The chief's voice is non-committal but his words test the steward's sudden silence like a traveler tests step by step an ice-bridge newly formed or sun-rotted too long by the spring.

"It was because of the messengers we let him live at first. When the messengers got back we thought we could then send the wretched vagabond home. That would have even satisfied the wretched hell-bent Chinaman—bearded talking Chinaman with his scolding. And all the Twelve Tribes—more, all the tribes of Amdo—would then be laughing at the earless rascal. Instead—."

The steward leans forward and draws his hearers' heads close together. As much as he can he is going to tell all. They will know soon anyway.

"—instead the messengers got back; five days ahead of time but with ruined horses, and said they could find no encampment or family by those names. Among the Gsar-ta Goloks—farthest of all the Goloks—there is no encampment of Ong-kor or family of Wan-dro."

No encampment—no family by those names! Then all that part of the tale was fictitious. What else was story or fable instead of fact? Parts—entire sections of that marvellous tale as though freshly spoken, sing in their minds, together with the questionings that come as the chief and his men grasp the full import of the steward's words, and finally gasp in unison,

"Then where was he born?"

"Whose son?"

The chief's voice seems to have changed as he says the last words. Or is it that the illusion of change is haunting the steward and he fancies things that have no basis in fact? But the fancy makes him reckless. To rout the hidden thoughts of others he brings out his own hidden thoughts.

"I don't care where he was born or whose son he is—even old Yzimba himself—. I could kill him with my own hands but the others are afraid. Now we dare not kill him, and we dare not let him go. If we let him go we admit his claim, and the others, the ombos and the Ram, dare not kill him. What are we to do with him? Yet maybe the Ngawa king will know what to do. He had many strange ideas when he was at the council but maybe with all those strange ideas he will know what to do. So I must go on without delay. I can't even stay this afternoon. Maybe the Ngawa king will know what to do so no one will laugh. I must go on."

The steward speaks as though to forestall a more pressing invitation to stay. But the chief does not urge anything as they rise and start back to camp. He has been sitting facing downstream and has seen a file of horsemen crossing the half-mile wide ford. Nam-jor the eldest son will be arriving with companions and there will surely be news.

The confusion of the steward's departure is followed not long after by the confusion of Nam-jor's arrival, yet it is after nightfall before all are finally gathered by the hearth fire in the great home tent of the chief for the hearing and telling of the news, after the evening meal is finished and the time for talk has come.

The chief slowly fills his silver mounted horn pipe and with the pincers that are tied to it fishes for a hot coal in the glowing ash pit of the fire. The pipe is the preliminary to speech and when he has finished it he will begin the session. But his son suddenly breaks the time-honored custom and speaks first.

"Who left here not so long before we arrived? Who went on and whither?"

"The Gurdu steward going to Ngawa."

It is as though speech passes between Nam-jor and his com-

panions—five young fellows from as many tribes gathered to make
a hunt together. A common idea as uniform as the fireglow that is
reflected from all their faces passes from eye to eye and lip to lip,
yet not a word is spoken until the chief questions.

"What is the news? What is it that everyone says by all the
fires that are lit between Sohk-tsong and Tahk Thzang Lhamo?
What do they say about the Gurdu affair?"

"The news father, is mostly what you have already heard—the
coming of the Chinese general and all that. But beyond any doubt
the Gurdu Lama bumped his head on the ground to the Chinese
officers. The ombos and the steward too. Then the general left
and after a few days all was as quiet as before, only it is rumored
that the general said that the Earless One—Om mani padme
hum—that he should be earless—is to be left alone. At least he is
now well-fed and well-treated. The general said he, the Earless
One, is under the protection of the "emperor's household" in
Nanking, wherever that is.

"The Chinese had a box that talks through space and he ordered the iron birds to bring bombs to drop on Gurdu unless the
Gurdu Great House submitted and tied the head to him. So they
gave him five good black horses and tied the head to him—Gurdu
Great House tied the head to a miserable Chinaman."

"Tell your father about the messengers. That is the best news
of all. Tell about the men who rode for fifteen days to seek a
phantom family in a ghost encampment."

One of the five can't refrain from this remark and immediately
goes on to tell the story himself.

"The encampment the Earless One—Om mani padme hum!—
told about among the Gsar-ta Goloks does not exist. There is no
encampment of Ong-kor, so there is no family of Wan-dro to have
a son who went on pilgrimage to Lhasa. Fifteen days' ride to find
an encampment which does not exist. It is a wonder they did not
kill him immediately when the messengers got back. But of course
the Chinese general had come in the meantime and had scolded
them well. Oh there is news—there is news of every kind. And
the Gurdu steward went to Ngawa, did he? He needs to go."

"That's the news but the jokes are better, by the presence of
the Buddha—yes the Gurdu Buddha, whichever one he is. The
lama knows—only the lama knows."

The young brave who takes up the tale rolls his eyes unabashed even by the stern set face of the chief.

"Gurdu has the strangest lamas. That is what we say in our tribe. They must like strange ones for they have two—oddities both. One has no ears and one worships the wretched Chinese. Don't be angry, chief. Gurdu after all is not your lamasery."

It has become a race for each one of the group to have his say; telling the things that make the tribesmen laugh. So yet another goes on.

"Ah, but listen to this. It is what the Ngawa king said when he was in Lhamo and now—yes now—the steward goes to the Ngawa king. He is a lamb for all of his dark black looks. The Ngawa king asked the Yellow Head to attend the council that tried the Earless One. He asked the Yellow Head to give his opinion and help choose the lama.

"You know the Yellow Head who lives in Lhamo and preaches another religion—the Yellow Head who is not of the faith of the Enlightened One. He asked him to speak the deciding word. But the Yellow Head only laughed. My brother was in the Yellow Head's guestroom and heard it all. Then the Yellow Head talked religion the way he does and preached of chosen saviors: a savior chosen by God and saviors chosen by men themselves. It was a good sermon, my brother said. He laughed when he told about it although at that time the men of our tribe had not as yet dared to laugh. But now since they looked among the Goloks for a family that does not exist, every one laughs.

"If the Earless One does not have a family then he must have dropped from heaven. So Gurdu has two lamas—a terrestrial one, the son of Thsa-ru-ma, and a celestial one dropped from heaven but found in a cave. Maybe they are twins. Even if they are twins I'd like to know if they have the same father. There are many such things I'd like to know. The lama knows—Om mani padme hum! Only the lama knows."

"What will Gurdu do?" The chief has finished his pipe and asks the question as he knocks out the ashes.

Nam-jor speaks up to answer with sudden emphasis. "It is no more what will Gurdu do, but what will Ah Ta the bold do. Unless of course the Earless One dies. He may die yet. But father, we do nothing more for Gurdu. It is too difficult and also too funny. Anyway, remember the gray horse.—"

The chief's warning hand stops him, yet that hand seems as

a signal for a wild burst of shouting outside. The great mastiffs, too, are baying through the night. But the noise dies away like gusts of ghostly laughter. It is only the usual alarms of the night, but to the chief it seems like the echo of the gusts of laughter blowing through the encampments of the Twelve Tribes. Even by his own fireside they are laughing again about the double lama—celestial and terrestrial.

His face changes in the fireglow. Then too, there is the matter, a long time ago, of the gray horse. Only his son and the headman who has said no word all evening know about that secret gift. Laughter long on the way is about to arrive. Yet something deeper than laughter comes into his face as he remembers the Earless One telling his tale. The tribesmen may laugh—and in time he among them—but that laughter is followed by the words "Om mani padme hum!" said in homage to the celestial manifestation of the Gurdu Lama. All are agreed that Gurdu has two lamas: the Earless One and the worshiper of The Wretched Chinese. With an irony that can never pass they add to their praying and their laughter the words,

"How fortunate is Gurdu Great House. The lama knows— only the lama knows."

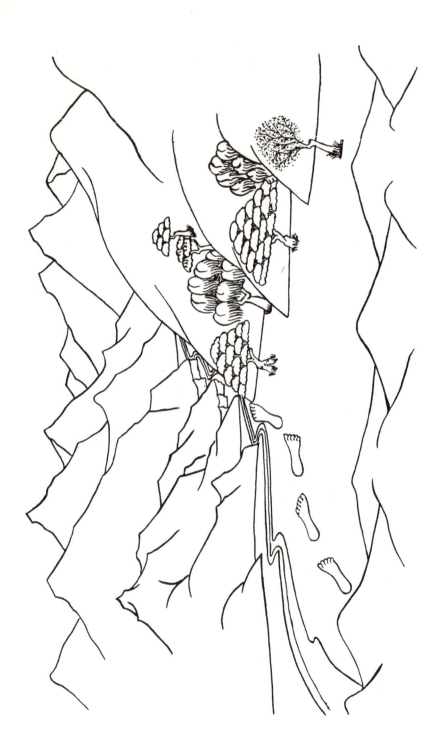

XIV

The forest covers the mountainside: an interwoven pattern of green, brown, and white, for the snow has newly blanketed the great spruces, green of branch and brown of trunk. The whole is gilded everywhere with patches of sunlight that the shadows stamp into a thousand lacy patterns as the sun climbs high in the sky. Ceaselessly the wind tries its will with the protesting trees but with the midday sun another sort of movement commences and bits of snow begin to slip from the branches: splattering through to the ground and dragging other tiny snowslides in their wake.

They sound like despairing exclamations of dismay to the one who crouches within the insufficient shelter of a great hollow tree. The slight heat that has loosened the snow is not enough to warm his cramped body and he does not dare start a fire. In fact it is as much to hide as to find shelter that he crouches so close within the tree. Yet he half knows that his hiding is in vain: all because of the tracks in the snow that lead away from the tree. Other track were all covered in the night but those are the ones left by one who went away in the half-light of the break of day and no snow has fallen since then.

Thus Aluk Shiang Cheung the Earless One hides on the third day of his escape. But that escape is not yet final. As he shifts his position there is the faint clink of metal touching metal, for he is still closely fettered with iron hobbles on his ankles. He is hiding in the heart of the forest beyond the first ridge of mountains that bound the Ngawa valley, yet fettered as he is he could not walk much farther than the nearest tree and so he can only hide. From time to time he tests a knife against his fetters; shaving off fine shreds of iron, for the knife is of the finest steel, but, for all of its edge, of little use for cutting through heavy iron hobbles.

The tracks that lead away from his hiding place have a strange

97

fascination for him and his gaze is on them incessantly; seeing in his thoughts how they lead, fateful and sure, through the forest till they reach the stream, cross it on the ice—looking darker than ever against that double whiteness—and then up the opposite slope to the pass and down somewhere into the Ngawa valley. There someone will see them. Surely someone will see them. Yet there was nothing else they could do.

The monk had to go back among people and find a file. Their last resource for opening the hobbles had been exhausted and further flight was impossible. Soon their food too would be finished. Yes, they had to have a file. But it was evil fortune that made it snow so heavily, making the countryside a blank page for the writing of a story: the story of one man's fidelity, courage and strength.

Many days have passed since the night the jailor of the Gurdu prison brought a full meal and an extra garment to the captive one. Each day thereafter he brought a full meal and the prisoner wondered more and more even as his strength returned. The wound on his back healed. The two wounds on the sides of his face became fresh red scars, and his feet seemed less numb under the weight of his fetters. But with a stronger physical grasp on life he came to a sharper realization of how very uncertain was his chance of life. One month for the messengers to go and come— maybe a few days less with the haste of their return trip when they knew—and then? His life would hang by a hair that the merest whim or fancy could cut. And he had a month. But the month passed and nothing of his captivity was changed.

But later when the steward came into his cell he knew that the messengers had returned at last, though it was many days later than he had first reckoned. However that might be it was, he thought, the end. At least that end would be fairly quick. Of that he was sure, for so he had judged the impatience and fear of the steward. But the steward ignored him completely as far as any outward sign was concerned, and only looked to the changing of the captive's fetters so he could be put on a saddle.

The Captive One found himself on a horse and learned it was the break of day. Guarded by a heavy force he rode westward and southward across the Southern Plain, still wondering just what had happened and curious as to what would happen.

Neither wonder nor curiosity showed in his face. Following

his speech in the lamasery he had reverted to his former defense of silence and since that day of surprising utterance had said nothing. Being the Silent One made him also appear in time like the Un-hearing One. The "Earless One," the members of the guard said to one another in joking whispers, and came to think of him as such; letting down the guard on their tongues. By the end of the second day he knew something about the visit of the Chinese general—at least insofar as it concerned him—and the whole story of the messengers' return. He also learned he was going to the Ngawa king but with that his information ended, for no one knew any more than that.

In the Mei Thzang—the palace of the Ngawa king—his capti-vity was much less close than it had been. In that enormous build-ing a wing or a floor might be almost isolated from the rest of the rooms and a prisoner could have a very fair amount of liberty. Actually, at times he was allowed the run of the entire second floor where the real life of the court went on and although heavily fettered could get from room to room. But in truth the treatment he received, the manner of his life, and most of all the attitude of the Ngawa king irked him more than the horrors of the cell in Lhamo. At Lhamo he had known just what to expect. He had known so exactly the feelings and reactions of his enemies that, with tolerable accuracy, he knew in advance what to expect and could forecast their action. But in the Mei Thzang he felt lost. He felt like one riding in the mist on the level trackless plain—in heavy mist when the wind has ceased to blow. And always, when-ever they met, the face of the Ngawa king matched his own in its expression of nothingness.

It came to be a relief to watch the face of the monk who served him and acted as guard: a simple face with wide smiling mouth and eyes of startled horror each time they noticed the two red scars of the Earless One.

"Om mani padme hum!"

Was it an exclamation or a prayer? Aluk Shiang Cheung knew it was a prayer the day his guard began to say, "With reverence—with reverence," yet glancing around fearfully lest someone had overheard. That half-unconscious backward look had first con-vinced the Aluk that it would be worthwhile, and he, the one who had refused every time but once to talk to ombos, chiefs, and even the king himself, spoke again and again to a simple smiling monk with enormous arms and wide shoulders of tremendous strength.

It was child's play for the voice which had charmed the council at Lhamo to cast a spell over the credulous monk, but it was something more than mere tricks of language and a persuasive tongue that made a convert. Aluk Shiang Cheung had always had a strange, almost hypnotic power over men. The monks of Drag Kar lamasery had felt that influence, the little acolyte had lost his life in sheer loyalty to the one he had chosen to follow from the very mouth of the Drag Kar cave, and Rgyal-wo Wang, weary aristocrat tired of all men, had yet been touched in some degree by that same influence. And it was surely one of the reasons why the Gurdu steward hated him so fearfully. Now that power claimed the allegiance of the monk who guarded him and won belief for the lama who first of all believed so completely in himself.

Only the face of the Ngawa king remained to trouble him: a face that matched his own in knowingness of expression. Sometimes the Earless One thought that the king knew everything, even to the plans for escape, yet that escape took place without a check. Only the matter of getting the key for the heavy fatters went wrong. Yet the escape was accomplished for all of that check. The monk carried him on his back through the night and maybe that single set of tracks threw the pursuers off, for the two were able to reach the shelter of the nearest wood before daybreak.

The second night was harder, for the country was rougher and the hillsides more steep. But the monk seemed tireless, though his great shoulders heaved and his breath blew like that of a loaded yak going uphill. But when daybreak found them far enough from Ngawa so they did not need to hide so closely, they knew also that the flight could not go on. All that day they worked at the locks and fetters, using stones and the very good knife the monk had filched from the king's own table, but at the end of the day the shackles were as tightly locked as before. "A file—a file—." The thought that had been struggling into being all day took form in words as they had to acknowledge defeat.

But the monk with unabated courage took up his burden for the third night.

"With reverence—with reverence," he would gasp as he climbed far up the mountainside of the great forest.

When daylight came he said he would go back to a distant village where he would get a file and with the words he left.

"With reverence—" so he bowed to receive a blessing and then was gone, but the tracks were left: black and fateful in the wood.

The Fettered One was left with his thoughts and his memories of the face of the Ngawa king. It haunts him with its certainty and its disdain, and as he sits and listens to the falling snow he wonders whether he has been outwitted. The single track in the snow will somehow furnish the answer. If at dusk or later the monk comes back along that track it will mean freedom, and with freedom whatever desperate action his scars and his memories prompt him to take. If however, others come along that track: hunters, riders, the men of Ngawa hunting the rarest of game, it will mean recapture and whatever of penalty and torture, if not of death, that will bring. But if neither come along that track he is trapped, and when his food is finished the story too is ended. Closely hobbled as he is he can never hope to follow the track and get anywhere. Then the story of Aluk Shiang Cheung is told.

Life and death are related to those marks in the snow. Little snowslides plummet from the branches of the trees and even fill some of the footprints yet they will never cover them entirely. Above the noise of the falling snow he listens for the sound of someone coming along the trail.

Then he hears them: riders coming over the pass and riding recklessly. The sound drops to the valley bottom, and then spreads along the streambed, where men are hobbling their horses before they start up on foot through the thick forest. He knows, long before they arrive, that his attempt to escape has failed.

They find him sitting—for all of his fetters—as a lama should sit, back to a great tree that is partly hollow. They find nothing else: neither food bag nor bowl, but they have found the Escaped One and their work is done. The Escaped One is the Recaptured One and that recapture is the story that men will now tell.

The tracks in the snow have betrayed him to his enemies, but who betrayed the monk and where is he now—the one of the broad back, sturdy limbs and brave heaving chest?

What does the face of the Ngawa king show at the sight of the Recaptured One, as their looks meet and clash?

XV

"Ku—hu—hu-hu! Up—up and look—up!"

The cry rises with the sudden breaking of the dawn, and nearly a score of men come out of sleep and the warm lairs of fleece
and felt they have made against the cold. The frosty night shivers
into a day partly veiled with shimmering hoar frost and light
snow that seems uncertain whether to fall or drift on. Everything
is blanketed with a thin white covering that is only broken into
dark trampled fragments where the horses stand, and more newly
where each white mound heaves like an opening grave to let a man
and rifle appear. Yet the horselines are intact: the horses coupled
with iron hobbles. Not a horse is missing, yet the cry is thrown
into the day.

"Ku—hu—hu-hu! Up—up and look—up!."

The prisoner is gone. Fifteen men of Ngawa—picked horsemen
and riflemen—stare blankly at one another and then at their leader
for there are no tracks, and the saddle blankets with a saddle for
a pillow that made a bed for the prisoner are as smoothly covered
as anything else. But he, the prisoner, is not there: he has been
gone since before it started snowing sometime in the dark hours.

The *ner-wa*, trusted officer of the Ngawa king, takes charge of
the confusion and his orders are sharp with a peculiar urgency.
The Escaped One must be found. He cannot be far away, for evidently he still has on iron hobbles—at least he did not leave them
in camp—so he cannot be far away. The camp boils with activity
as horses are unhobbled and saddled, and in a very short time the
pursuit is ready: horses stiff with cold and with knotted tails held
high, whirling and trying to get their heads. Certainly the prisoner
can be caught for the pursuit can comb the countryside in a radius
too wide to let a fugitive on foot get away even if he were not
hobbled.

The bivouac is in a wide valley where flat meadows border Bird Waters, a stream halfway between swimming water and fordable, but now uniformly white under snow-covered ice. Downstream the valley widens to a long, low line in the distance: a brush-dotted plain where Bird Waters joins Peacock Waters, but upstream high mountains show darkly through the snow, and the valley sides climb in smooth curves to a wavy skyline. For miles all is open as the palm of one's hands with not a hiding place in sight.

"Ku—hu—hu-hu—ku-hu-hu!"

The echoes die away as the tracks of sixteen horses are unrolled in an ever-widening circle; spreading a dark tangled pattern across the snow. The hunt is on and soon should end for the picked horsemen of Ngawa are looking for a lone fugitive who at best must be limping with a heavy iron hobble still clamped to one ankle. Yet as they ride, with assured success before them, the men of Ngawa are still conscious of vague misgivings coupled with self-blame, and they whisper to each other in a confused chorus.

"It was not good—not good that we did not watch: even if he was hobbled and so sick. Not good that we did not watch."

"Ah, the *aku ner-wa* will find it hard to tell why he did not set a watch. What will Mei Rgyal-wo say when he hears that the Earless One escaped?"

"But how did he do it? He was hobbled and so sick."

"The lama knows. By the Precious Magic there are things I do not understand. Yes, things I do not understand. The lama knows."

Maybe there are things he too does not understand, yet the *ner-wa* rides with his head held high; his keen glance taking in all the landscape—white and unreal through the snow fog. Somewhere in all that wide open country his prisoner, now free or partially free, hides or flees. If he flees he is now leaving tracks and if he hides he cannot be far away. Following an order, the pursuit fans out to comb every hollow or irregularity of terrain. The men ride more slowly, searching with new care for the Earless One. So the hunt goes on.

It is something more than two months since the Earless One sat at the foot of a great tree—partly hollow—and watched his captors come through a forest draped with snow. From that tree he was taken back to the Mei Thzang but nothing of added punishment or penalty was imposed. He held his resolution stiff to suffer and nothing happened, and after a time his resolution tired of the strain. As before his attempt to escape, he had a certain degree of freedom and his food was unchanged both in quantity and quality. Two monks served him instead of one but he talked with neither one of the two for they were always together. No one told him what had become of his former keeper: he of the broad shoulders and willing constant strength.

For two months he did not see the Ngawa king except for that single exchange of glances when he was first brought back. Most of the time the king was away on his own concerns but when he was home the prisoner never saw him. Always he had the feeling that he was playing with an invisible antagonist who had scored the last point and gained an advantage. A thousand times he wished he had never attempted escape—an escape which had ended in neither freedom nor death. Even captivity had no pains on which to whet his resolution, or against which to pit his silence.

He remained silent even when brought before the young king as a culprit is brought before a judge. Yet the king asked no questions and never ordered him to answer: never shouted at him a command to "speak!": an order that could only echo emptily in the far reaches of his mocking silence. The king talked only; telling him that the time during which he might have pled for mercy and made peace was up. The time of probation in Ngawa, where neither mistreatment nor death would ever come to him, had come to an end. He must go back to Gurdu where anew the Tebbus demanded that he be cut to pieces with slow carefulness.

"You the Earless One—" the words were disdainful and insulting, yet the voice was oddly detached, "who call yourself the Gurdu Lama, must go back to Gurdu. Neither my mercy nor the power of the Chinese can protect you now. I am through and the Chinese general is far away—very far away in Chinese country." The king's voice was mocking yet quiet.

"The lama who seeks to know what lama he is was marvelous when he spoke to all the tribes in the Great House at Lhamo. And Gurdu had helped him by cutting off his ears. If they had let him escape it would have been much easier. If only they had left him his ears it would have been easiest of all. But the lama who could ride the air on a spirit horse by reason of the Precious Magic could only be carried by another when he sought to flee. And he rode another's back but a short distance. Well that is all, only you who call yourself the Gurdu Lama go back to Gurdu to die."

The words were final: the judgment was given. The Ngawa king was one who had never been known to go back on his word. Yet to the prisoner the words sounded unreal. He had once heard the threats of those who hated him utterly and this calmly spoken sentence seemed artificial. Yet for what of reality did he wait as he listened on, for what should yet be said, or was it that he waited for that which should be left unsaid? The Ngawa king, signaling that the meeting was ended, said yet one more thing.

"You die, Aluk Shiang Cheung—unless indeed you escape a second time by dint of long practice; not by reason of the Precious Magic but by dint of long practice making shift to escape. But this time remember the file—remember the file."

There is hidden laughter in the words—a laughter more cruel than blows. With the words the prisoner is led from the room.

Sixteen men—picked men and picked rifles—rode with him from Ngawa to take the Earless One to his doom. Compared with the carelessness of the hundred horsemen who had brought him from Gurdu their vigilance and efficiency was a seamless, flawless thing and made a prison from which there could be no escape.

Perfect guards though they were they yet talked as they rode or sat around the noonday fire, and from that talk he learned a piece of news that was partly reassuring yet also a part of the things he could not understand: things hidden in the mysterious inscrutability of the king of Ngawa. The monk who had guarded him: he of the broad shoulders and the brave loyal heart had not been punished. At least no punishment of which anyone knew had been given. The monk had not even been beaten when he had been caught in the blacksmith shop trying to steal a file.

He had, however, been sent away but not as an exile. That, too, was surprising. Many a man who has incurred the wrath of the king is sent away—noseless, earless, or lacking one hand—to beg his way among the village folk, but the monk had been given the means to go on pilgrimage and was now, so every one thought, halfway to Lhasa. That the one who had carried him for three nights had come to no harm was a comforting thought to the prisoner but because he could not reason out the motive the fact yet filled his mind with a vague unease.

The latter half of the day saw the party over the snow-filled pass of Jamtso La, but also found the captive so sick he could hardly keep his horse, and camp was made long before well-mounted men traveling from Ngawa to Gurdu on a mission that would not wait should have stopped. But the flats of the upper Bird Waters valley offered a fair stand of winter-killed, snow-bleached hay, and the night began rosy with the afterglow. All the stars too came out, but the weather-wise veterans of thousands of nights in the open smelled snow in the air and talked about it as they sat around the fire. The captive was not in that ring around the fire although his place had been fixed as for an honored guest. He had eaten nothing since noon and lay silent and apathetic where they had made his bed. Yet to the men who tried to get him to eat and who watched, this silence was filled with a groaning more real than sound. He was a very sick man and they wondered whether they might not come to turn back without ever having to go on to Gurdu.

Could it be that the *ner-wa* and his fifteen companions were to be the witnesses of the final act? Were they to see the end of the feud? Was the final answer to the question which had split all of Amdo into two increasingly hostile camps to be given, and the verdict rendered, on the flats of the upper Bird Waters valley, in sight of Peacock Waters now covered with intermittent icebridges? They could not know, but everything about the captive suggested death. He who had outfaced the wrath of Gurdu, the torture and hardships of the most vindictive captivity, and all the dangers of his life as a claimant lama, was dying while they looked on.

They talked about it in whispers as they sat around the fire, though they were convinced that the prisoner could not have heard it if they had shouted instead. They talked about something else, too, though the *ner-wa* had locked great iron hobbles on the ankles of one who knew nothing about it. It seemed a senseless thing but the *ner-wa* would take no chances, though he argued the other matter with his men.

"No, enough to make our faces smart. That we the men of Ngawa should set a guard over our horses while we are still in Ngawa territory is the dreaming of a crazy man. Even the miserable Chinese turn their horses free at night in this one district of all the districts of Amdo, thanks to our king's word and law. We need not watch our horses, and certainly we need not watch the prisoner. We set no watch when we, the men of Ngawa, camp on our doorstep. By the ears of the lama, no. Ah, the poor Earless One. Maybe though we should watch him to see the end. It is the poison gas of Jamtso La that has done this. Will he go honorifically into the zenith before us—faster than our horses can go, or will he travel with us till we come to the Gurdu Great House? The lama knows."

The stars looked down on a sleeping camp where nothing stirred, and then came the snow to shut the eyes of even the stars.

"Ku-hu-hu-hu—ku-hu-hu—."

The hunter-warriors' cry echoes more and more faintly over the flats and meadows at the confluence of Peacock Waters and Bird Waters. The hunt goes on at full speed: the horses racing across the snow with their knotted tails held straight behind them. Among all the inexplicable and unanswerable things that fill their minds, fifteen men yet think mostly of the words of the *ner-wa* when he ordered no watch to be set. And he, the sixteenth rider, the *ner-wa* who will have to render account to the Ngawa king, rides with his head held high looking for sign of the Escaped One: not yet honorifically gone into the zenith leaving no tracks, yet mysteriously gone somewhere leaving no tracks.

XVI

The headman of the Sohk-tsong chief carefully sets his brimming bowl on the edge of the ashpit and dips his fingertips in the melted butter that floats on the hot tea. With them he cleans his face and the creases around his eyes, wiping away the dust and grime that cling like a mask, for he has been riding far in one of the furious dust storms that sweep the plain of Sohk-tsong in late winter. The wind, tearing with savage fingers at the fences and wattle walls of the winter encampment, finding a way even into the sod and plaster hut of the chief, and bringing dust to mix with the smoke that drifts from the half-dead hearth fire, whines like a living creature balked of its prey, for the headman can now wipe his eyes—red-rimmed and smarting—and stare silently at the chief. There is much he has to say, if the wind will let him say it, but first he must eat and drink and for that silence is best.

In the hut, too, silence is best even after he has licked out his bowl and replaced it within the folds of his great sheepskin coat, so the two go out again into the wind that bites at their heels, tearing dust and ash from their footsteps and flinging it in long gray shreds along the course of the storm. Followed by the gray mastiffs that march like a guard at their heels, the two climb the ash and refuse heap that rises like a miniature volcanic cone of cinders and ash in front of the chief's hut. Sitting there with their heads together, they begin to talk, sure that their words are only heard by themselves, though the great mastiffs lift their ears with a half-human interest.

"By the Books, I was not the only one who was traveling among the tribes to find out what was happening. I met Slab Face Rinchen come from the Archu chief, and Stretch Ears Jamtzen come from the Sechu Great House—also many others—all traveling to find out the price of one thing and another. I was asking the price of wool, you remember.

"After the attempted escape the first time everyone had begun to laugh. The lama knows how everyone laughed—we too—to think of the Earless One carried like a bag of grain for three days and then found still hobbled like a stray horse—he of the Precious Magic and strange powers who could read the future. Ah, the Ngawa king is a wise one. Wise—yes, very wise. The tribesmen laughed and they forgot for a time the story of his pilgrimage to Lhasa and maybe they even began to forget about the Chinese general and the other lama who worships the miserable strangers."

"As we seemed to forget the Earless One, or forget at least the things about him that made him great, so in Lhamo they began to forget the Chinese general and the orders he gave about the captive. The steward was in that, they say. He visited among the Tebbus, and then the Tebbus came and demanded that the captive be brought back from Ngawa and be given to them. The miserable Tebbus—dirt-grubbing wretches—are bloody-minded. Om mani padme hum!"

The speaker stops and stares thoughtfully at the scene before them: a winter landscape turning sick with the thaws and dust storms of spring. Yellow and white and dreary, the plains and the ice-covered rivers and streams lie under the dim flat horizon. Close to the encampment dust devils spring into a dizzy dance and leap at them to the shrill whistling of the wind. Against that shrill insistence he forces his words; speaking directly into the chief's ear.

"Ever since the Earless One was sent to Ngawa, Ah Ta the bold has been missing—away from Rzachdumba—no one knows where. For over two months there has been no communication between Gurdu and Rzachdumba.

"Gurdu had a great cursing service and the horsemen who carry the curse rode to throw it in Rzachdumba territory but were fired on by Rzachdumba scouts and had to turn back too soon. That was a failure. The image of the curse was made that time without ears, but when the riders had to drop it before reaching the boundary hilltop, the curse bounced back. A curse is like a gun that shoots both ways.

"At last, however, Gurdu Great House decided to forget about the Chinese government and Ah Ta the bold—to forget everything but its vengeance on the flesh and bones of the one already made earless. So they sent to Ngawa for the prisoner."

"Why?"

The sharp monosyllable of the chief's question broke for a moment the steady flow of the headman's speech.

"Why? To kill him, to be sure. But when the tribesmen heard that he was going to die they stopped laughing about the Earless One and began again to say "The lama knows. Om mani padme hum!" The Tebbus came to Lhamo—nine hundred of them— sharpening their swords so each one could cut a little strip from the flesh of the one who calls himself Aluk Shiang Cheung—Lama of Gurdu Great House.

"All this has been easy to learn, for I have been in Lhamo it- self, but about what really happened in Ngawa no one knows. On the first night out from Ngawa, when lying heavily fettered with great iron hobbles in the midst of the best warriors of the Mei Thzang—men who awake when a horse changes his breath- ing—he escaped. Some say there were sentries set and some say there were none. It snowed that night yet he left no tracks. At daybreak sixteen horsemen—and what horses they have in Ngawa— rode over all that country clear to Peacock Waters; country where a rabbit could find no place to hide, country as clean as our own meadows, and failed to find him. He had been sick the night be- fore and hobbled. He took the hobbles with him. How it was done no one knows."

"Precious Magic—The lama knows—Precious Magic—by the Books."

The chief's face is more intent than ever and the words are uttered more like thought escaped into speech than as conscious comment.

"Maybe—maybe. Certainly it is strange no tracks were found. Yet the next day the lama was seen on the other side of Peacock Waters by a Chu-ka-ma shepherd. The shepherd was at his fire when the lama climbed out of a nearby watercourse and passed— the lama—"the speaker's voice falters and stops in confusion "—at least they call him a lama. Everyone calls him a lama."

The Sohk-tsong chief's grim set face does not change but he nods as though giving permission, and his headman goes on with his tale.

"The lama passed only a short distance from the fire but never looked toward the fire nor spoke. He walked with a limp and held

one end of the iron hobbles in his left hand for it was still fastened
to his left ankle. Yet he walked fast and never looked toward the
fire even when the shepherd called to him. Then the shepherd ran
after him and though the lama never seemed to hurry he had to run
a distance to catch up to him. He begged him to go back and
drink at his fireside but the lama refused. He said, 'I make no one
black—I who am black with the guilt that Gurdu, Ngawa, and
Thsa-ru-ma have put upon me will not blacken you, poor shepherd. Anyway I do not need what you give and must hurry on my
way. My destiny is calling me.'

"That is what the Earless One said—for it was he. He took off
his hat when he spoke of his destiny and the shepherd saw that
his ears were missing, so he knew that he was the Earless One
escaped. It was a dangerous thing to know and the shepherd said
nothing about it for days. Chu-ka-ma is so close to Ngawa they
dare not incur the wrath of the Ngawa king. So he kept a still
mouth until all the world knew and was talking about it, even
though he had not given tea to the fugitive. Yes, he really is escaped. The shepherd of Chu-ka-ma is not the only one who has seen
him."

It is hard to tell a secret in the teeth of such a wind as threat-
tens to shave off layer by layer the top of the ash-heap. But at
least no one can eavesdrop—no one except the dogs that wait for
the end as though they too were involved and really understood.

"But are you sure he was not again made prisoner by Chu-ka-
ma or Wad-ma and is secretly held or maybe has even been killed?
Maybe they let him escape so he could be killed and it would
never be known. Even the Chinese general could no longer blame
in such a case. The Ngawa king is wisest of all the rulers of Amdo.
Are you sure...?"

The chief does not finish his sentence but searches the other's
face for a refutation of his fears.

"I am sure he got away. I saw one of the hunters of Wad-ma
who saw him two days later. They were in the hilly country between Wad-ma and Ngura—quite a large party of them—and they
saw a dust-devil dancing up the trail. When it came near they saw
that a man moved within: a man wearing a yellow robe and a great
Golok hat—a hat terribly ragged and stained."

" 'Lags-so. The Lama knows, Lags-so' they greeted him.
'Where does the Presence go and how?' They could see he was a

great lama by the way the dust-devil stayed with him when he stood still and they added, 'But let us lend you a horse: we lead extra ones.'

"The lama did not answer at first but looked at the blue sky and took off his hat. Then they saw that his ears were gone. Yet from where his ears had been light leaped like the flames of a wood fire on a dark night. It was the Earless One and so they knew for the first time that he had escaped for they had seen no one else for five days.

"'Lags-so, the Lama knows, Lags-so,' they said and again offered a horse, but the Lama answered:

"'I do not need it. My destiny takes me where I need to go, be it easy or hard, and the winds learn to follow me. However, my blessing on you. Brave sons, may your hunting be good.'

"He went on and they tried to follow but the wind swirled at his heels—leaping from footprint to footprint—till it lifted him in the air and their horses were running to keep up. But at the pass he went on so fast in the whirling dust-devils that their horses could no longer follow. His appearance was somewhat different from the time when he was seen by the Chu-ka-ma herder. He had no hobbles on his ankle nor did he carry any in his hand. Om mani padme hum! He is certainly a great magician for on that day the hunters killed more game than on all the other days of their hunt put together. And that night there was a strange sky with the light that flames in the north. In that sky they saw two ears of light hung like a sign."

"Still he is earless, the lama knows—by the ears of the lama he lacks."

The chief was arguing some secret debate with himself and the words slipped out inadvertently, yet he rolled his shoulders so the collar of his coat rubbed against his own ears. The feel of them was reassuring.

"Ah, chief, but wait. Hear what happened in Ngura, for there is where he entered into the dwellings of men. There the Ngawa king no longer has any power, so he was safe, and his hosts, who-ever they might be, were safe too. At the tent of the Ngura ruler he blessed all who came; telling them of a new hope for all who believed in him. When he had finished blessing them he took off his hat and where they had before seen two red scars they saw ears—lama's ears golden like those of a golden idol. Later he again put on his hat and then took it off and the ears were gone.

"'I am the Earless One,' he said, and again blessed the people."

"He is still in Ngura?"

"I don't know, chief. Nor does anyone else. He talked of the Black Tents, and Labrang, and China, and his destiny. It may be he is still in Ngura or at least just beyond the Peacock Waters on the way to the Sohkwo. The people of that region do not fear the Ngawa king. At any rate it will be easy to find him."

"Which is our best gray horse? Do we have one like the gray we sent two years ago to the north?"

The chief's face is as stern and set as ever. Once it was stern and set with indecision at the trial of a culprit, then it changed and broke with laughter, and now again it is stern and set—this time with a new decision.

"One like his twin brother, chief. When shall I start?"

"Quietly—quietly—with a small heart. What would happen to a small tribe like ours that is so near to Ngawa if the Ngawa king knew about the other gray horse? And now this one?"

"Ah, but chief, I have forgotten to tell the strangest news of all. The Ngawa *ner-wa* and his fifteen men have never been punished. Not even a single fine was levied. It was from out their hands that the Earless One escaped and they were not punished. What can be stranger than that? What can one say? The lama knows—."

The chief can say nothing. Strange things are taking place—have taken place—and now somewhere in the north country the Earless One follows his destiny. The chief knows only one thing at a time. This time it is that the Earless One shall follow that destiny on a great gray horse of Sohk-tsong, for maybe destiny will lead again to the Gurdu Great House.

The chief, gazing out over the flats—now dreary with a winter already passed and a spring not yet begun—has one more question to ask before he is ready to go back to the winter hut.

"Where is Ah Ta the bold?"

But no one has an answer to that question for no one knows about Ah Ta the bold.

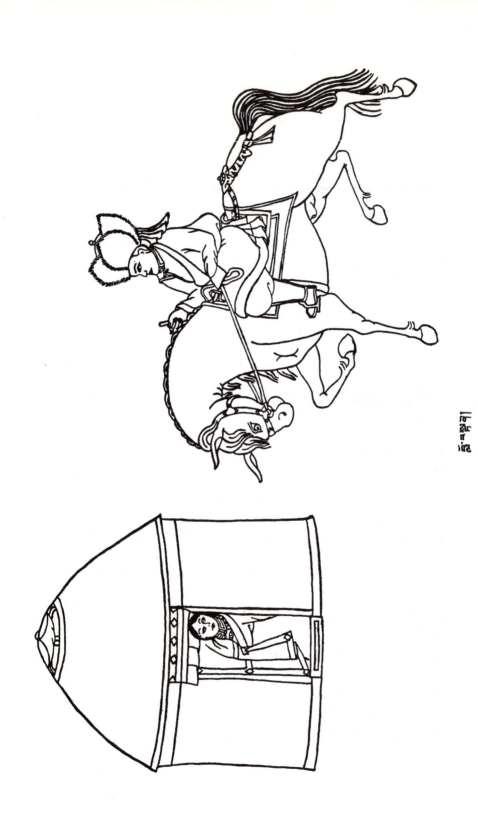

XVII

The star-studded curtain of the night stretches to the flat horizon: a faintly luminous backdrop against which is blacked in the
dim silhouette of the tents and herds of the Rgyal-wo Wang's encampment. The dark outline is not altogether black for fitful flashes of fireglow leak through curtained tent doors and under flapping
tent walls, and scores of shifting points of light glow in the night as
the cattle turn startled eyes toward those fireflashes. Only the
yurt of Aluk Shiang Cheung is entirely dark: a black cone giving
no sign; alien to life—blotting out some of the stars.

Faint sounds drift in on the night wind: the clink of snaffle
bits, the ring of stirrups that touch, the thud of hoofbeats and the
encampment dogs awake to their eternal vigil. A furious clamor
sweeps the encampment—to the very rim and beyond—yells,
gunfire, and voices far and near shouting in question and answer,
to end in a sudden wild hallooing.

"Aluk Shiang Cheung—Aluk Shiang Cheung!"

The drum roll beat of hooves when horses go at full speed, the
whine and crack of whirling whips, the startled yelping of some
dog that rushes too close—all swell like a torrent in spate on
which to question and answer ring out again with the shout.

"Aluk Shiang Cheung—Aluk Shiang Cheung!"

The dark shadow of the yurt is split in two by a shaft of light
that pours through the suddenly opened door, for a great fire of
coals burns in a brazier and fills the interior with fireglow—the
promise of comfort against the cold and the dark. The light is
blocked for a moment by a figure in the doorway: a woman with
braids that hang from her head like a shawl and with one arm and
shoulder suddenly bare in her haste, and then as the light again
pours unchecked through the open door and out across the encampment it seems to catch and hang on the long head and point-

115

ed ears of a great horse that comes along the beam of light to the very door of the yurt—his startled eyes gleaming like spotlights in the dark. Wan Chen Mtso is at the horse's head and her hands are upon the bridle as she hears a well-remembered voice saying,

"Food and drink for all in the home tent. Drink well, everyone, and tend well the horses."

A moment later Aluk Shiang Cheung has entered the yurt. Wan Chen Mtso follows and closes the door behind her, the felt curtains fall into place, and the encampment, the dogs, and the riders who mill around in confusion, finding place for their horses and their tasks, are all a part of the dark night, and outside. In that night the yurt too, is dark and silent—a black cone alien to life.

But within is a small world of little things—rich and well-kept—and two people face each other in the fireglow. The rugs of the lama's sleeping place are smoothly spread, and at his pillow is the wooden box of precious writings and special charms. His prayer wheel is in place and on the edge of the brazier a rare Ming bowl is set beside the butter box and a bag of fine Russian leather, sewn with fancy stitching: the lama's special pouch of tsamba that is freshly made each day. From the spout of the kettle a wisp of steam rises like a breath of winter, for the tea is ready: has been ready a long time.

Aluk Shiang Cheung sees none of these things, not even a silver-trimmed Russian rifle on the rack above his bed where his other rifle always hung, and beside it the polished case of a big Mauser pistol like the one the acolyte had carried and had tried to use with ready speed too late. In all that tiny world of fireglow and things rich and well-appointed he only sees a woman kneeling beside the brazier to cut shavings of butter into a Ming bowl.

So she cut butter into his bowl the first time he sat as a guest in the great tent of Rgyal-wo Wang, and again once when the world was narrowed to the circle of a tiny camp on a windswept hilltop. So times without number she had prepared his bowl while something of compelling power—deeper than words can sound—pulsed between them: pride, passion, and surrender all in one.

With his eyes fixed on that kneeling figure with the busy hands, Aluk Shiang Cheung, with infinite deliberation, takes off his great fox fur hat that has bonneted his head down to his shoulders. A dark red scarf—knotted under his chin—remains, and his fingers begin to fumble with that knot.

The busy hands falter and leave their task half done, and the tea in the kettle sings on unpoured, for Wan Chen Mtso can only watch those fingers till the knot is loosened. Then in her eyes there gleams a horrified reflection of what she sees as the scarf comes away: a head long and grotesquely top heavy bulges above cheek bones that seem to spread far beyond the familiar limits of the face, for beside them there are only two swellings of puckered skin and livid scar to tell of something missing. It is the face of the golden god distorted and strangely unfamiliar that is turned toward her, and from that mutilated setting eyes that too seem changed question her face—a face lit like a burnished mirror by the red glow of the burning coals.

The horror and strange unwilling repulsion in that face make an answer of a sort to the question in his eyes and they change again. They are the eyes of a stranger; asking for nothing, and far away. He seats himself on his bed.

"Pour the tea."

Her hands take up the unfinished task and the brimming bowl is held to him, as an offering is made, by two hands that are none too steady. But Aluk Shiang Cheung's voice as he talks between sips of tea, taken slowly, is even and steady—cold as ice that melts.

"Since I last was here I have been on a journey of many months and have been much delayed. I went as you know to Gurdu Great House and in Gurdu Great House my back was burned and I lost my ears, but that was not the end. I spoke words to the assembled leaders of the Twelve Tribes and the Tebbus but that was not the end. I went to Ngawa and lived in the Mei Thzang till I was carried like a sack of grain, and I sat under a tree in the forest of tumbling snow, but that was not the end. I went back to the lair of the Ngawa king and traveled with sixteen of his trusted warriors but that was not the end. I left them, in the night of falling snow, and crossed the icebridges of Peacock Waters, but that was not the end. I crossed the plains of Chiaokoh and walked with the wind among the hills of Ngura till I came to their tents, but that was not the end. I stayed in Ngura, in Nyin-ma, in Chu-ka-wei-shiong, in Ta-tzen, in Ko-tze; in each place waiting till my destiny should call, and then I came to the encampment of Rgyal-wo Wang among the Sohkwo, where is pitched the tent of Aluk Shiang Cheung, but that is not the end. That is not the end.''

The time is accounted for. Events and scenes have been made to fill the days that have intervened, and now he is back in his tent to take up life or follow his destiny. In casual fashion he goes on to ask news of the herds and of his affairs: how the milch cows are doing and what is the yield of lambskins from the spring crop of lambs. He can ask, too, for news; whether messengers have come from Labrang, if Chinese have come asking for Aluk Shiang Cheung, or whether Ah Ta the bold has sent him word?

His measured speech fills the little world within the yurt, and Wan Chen Mtso's replies are timely as she tells him all he wishes to know, but her eyes never leave off from a steadfast regard that seems to impose its own penalty. They begin to fill with fear. That she has lost the ears of her god—like a golden image in his beauty—seems horror enough, but a fear that she may lose yet more begins to grow and darken in her eyes. She can lose maybe the eyes of one who stares so strangely, she can lose maybe possession of those shoulders of which she has such immediate need; she can lose perhaps that spirit that says so calmly with a voice that turns her limp, ''But that is not the end—that is not the end.'' For as he talks he is going farther and farther away to that distant country of his pride. In her eyes that are nailed by agony to that place his ears have been, horror gives place to fear.

The red coals in the brazier shrink away, one from the other, and put on gray shrouds of ash before they die. So too, the light fades and the shadows grow thicker and darker around the sleeping place of the lama: around the figure, too, of the lama; hiding his hands, his shoulders, hiding indeed all but his face. Out of assured silence—he has learned all that he wants to know and has ceased from questioning—he again speaks.

''I am going to sleep. You can put the brazier a little nearer the door as you leave.''

The brazier and the door are the concrete objects of that sharp command, but the order is to leave. Wan Chen Mtso's fingers are obedient to take the brazier—but the door? And to leave? Even— she opens the door, but it is to set the brazier outside and fill the night with the red and sudden sign of life and activity at the yurt of Aluk Shiang Cheung—aloof and alien to life no longer.

She herself turns back into the yurt. In that darkened interior there is no longer a mutilated god, but her man whom she dares not leave, and fears to lose, with a fear that transcends all else. He is hers in the darkness—he himself, his shoulders and all—but as her hands find too those puckers of wrinkled skin and swollen scar, her whole body is shaken by sobs she can't control though her teeth clamp hard on a shoulder for comfort. So she unburdens herself of the pity even her eyes did not show, and then her sobbing must give way a little so she can plead, for one favor from the man who holds her in the dark.

"When—when you get back to Gurdu Great House you—you will let me—me and no one else—use the knife as I wish on the Gurdu ombo? Me and no one else? You promise me this? You eat the deadly curse that it will be?"

"When I go back to Gurdu Great House," answers the Earless One and her sobbing comes to an end.

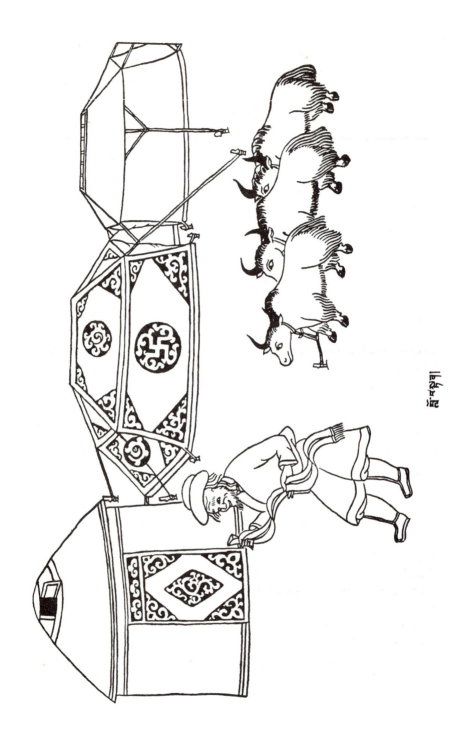

ᠲᠡᠷᠭᠡ

XVIII

An old man—the onetime horse herder for Gurdu now instal-led in the tent of Aluk Shiang Cheung—stands uncertainly outside the closed door of the lama's yurt, and awaits permission to enter.

So he has stood many times in the days just passed. The first time it was a Golok who had come—fifteen shaggy-headed riders with him—to demand audience with Aluk Shiang Cheung. That was a month ago and he has not as yet seen him. But the Golok, for all his rude oaths, is patient, and has camped on the meadow that stretches from the edge of the encampment to the edge of the stream. He has said he must see the Aluk Shiang Cheung and so he awaits the pleasure of the lama while his companions scanda-lize the Sohkwo by hunting marmots all day long.

His modest camp of two travel tents is not, however, the only camp on the flats. There are the pretentious and well-appointed tents of the Labrang envoy and his party. He is a great ecclesias-tic, official representative of the greatest lamasery in Amdo, but he too has waited many days to see Aluk Shiang Cheung, and so far has waited in vain. Still he does not leave but awaits the pleas-ure of the One Who is Never Seen—the Lama of the closed yurt.

Day by day the spread of tents along the edge of the stream increases. A delegation from Ngura is there, the fat chief of Tang Kur—wiliest diplomat among all the Twelve Tribes—is camped there too, and the ombo of Aluk Kong Thang Tsang has even set up a small yurt evidently expecting to stay a long time. Men of consequence are there from Chu-ka-wei-shiong, Ta-tzen, and Wei Tse; from Larengo, Amchok, and Samtsa; tribes free from the domination of Gurdu and Ngawa. Each group has its own fire and kettle and all are waiting for audience with the Lama of the closed yurt.

There are others more discreet or anonymous who keep to

themselves and proffer a score of reasons for being in the region. But they speak, when they talk at all, in the speech of the peoples of the great plains where the tribes are under the influence of Gurdu. Making furtive camps they seem hardly even to wait, and yet they stay on day by day.

At some distance from the others is a camp of five small tents different from all the rest. They are uniform—all but one— in style and size and are pitched in strict alignment. But that camp is meant for a parade ground or a city square, not for this mountain meadow of Amdo, and appears oddly awkward and ill at ease. Its self-conscious order gives no assurance of comfort, the tents sag sadly in the wind, and indeed the Chinese officer who camps there with his bodyguard is uncomfortable enough. But he, too, has come to see Aluk Shiang Cheung and must stay until that meeting is achieved.

The most recent camp is also the largest, for the good-sized ring of tents farthest downstream is where Ah Ta the bold has made his camp—one hundred and fifty riflemen with him. He came just yesterday, and the old man, announcing the arrival of Ah Ta the bold had been sure that he would be allowed to see Aluk Shiang Cheung without delay, yet the answer had been the same for him as for all the others.

"Tea and food in the great tent for all, and see that the camp they make is well supplied with fuel. When I am ready to receive him I will let him know."

Something of all this floats in the old man's mind as he stands at the door of the yurt waiting even his chance to speak to the One Who Is Never Seen. Once long ago the door of the yurt was almost never closed, but open to all: an audience hall that was never empty. Now behind that closed door is a shrine or a grave. Each time he waits for the signal to enter, the old man finds the yurt the place of a new mystery. Or is it that someone seeks to unravel a mystery already old and wearisome in its age, and would be undisturbed? This time the announcement he must make is ridiculous and foredoomed to refusal. When all those great ones—the Chinese officer and Ah Ta—have been refused, what chance is there? Almost the old man is about to turn away but the insistence of one man keeps him there waiting. The ragged monk had been so insistent. At the signal he pushes on the door and stands before the One Who Is Never Seen.

He wears a lama's hat. Even in the interior of his own yurt sitting on the rugs that make his bed he wears a lama's hat: yet a hat made somewhat differently from any lama's hat ever seen before. And wearing it he is no longer the Earless One but a lama enthroned and mitered with a miter that covers all the head. Each time in the last month that the old man has seen him he has been wearing the same hat. The Earless One is on the way to become the One Who is Never Seen and to that one—with bent back and palms spread wide in ample respect—the old man speaks.

"With respect—the Lama knows—with respect. There is a monk—a poor traveler on foot with a pack—who insists on speaking to the Aluk—with respect."

Each time before the lama's eyes, turning disdainfully, have shown no interest; even when it was Ah Ta the bold who had come. But this time they widen slightly; seeming to turn inward on some new thought that is worth their while.

"Let him have tea and food in the great tent. And then he can go on his way. Only fill well his food bag."

As he closes the door and leaves, the old man is uncomfortably certain of two things. The monk will not go: will not even be satisfied to stay on in the big tent without having seen the One Who Is Never Seen, and the Lama certainly will not see the monk. Yet in spite of this second certainty he is soon back at the door of the yurt awaiting permission to enter. The monk is so insistent: has said such strange things. That insistence dominates the old man and although he fears with a deep fear what the Lama may say yet he cannot help himself, he is back waiting for the signal to enter.

"With respect—the lama knows—with respect."

The words seem to do nothing or mean nothing, and yet it is all he knows how to say when his hands are turned palms outward and his back is bent as one would worship.

"With respect—the lama knows—."

His throat is dry for the lama's eyes begin to gleam strangely but always there is the memory of that insistent monk.

"He still insists he must see the Presence—he, the monk who will not leave. He also sends a present. With respect—strangest present I ever did see—with respect. This—the lama knows."

In his hands, held like one holds a charm or talisman to ward away the Lama's wrath, is a small three-cornered file, worn beyond any usefulness but a file nevertheless. It is his only excuse for his entrance into the yurt. He was told to show it and all would be well, so he shows it, and believes not at all that all will be well—in fact is certain that all is not well. He has seen before that gleam in the Lama's eyes and it always meant trouble. Now—. But the Lama speaks.

"Tell him, the monk of the broad shoulders, to come and see me. Let him come alone."

The old man is gone; wondering in a dazed way how the One Who Is Never Seen Knows how broad the monk's shoulders really are. He has left the door open in his haste. The monk is not yet come but all the world without comes through that open door: the sound of the Goloks shouting along the stream, the barking of the dogs, the murmur of chanting in the Labrang envoy's tent, and the sound of splashing water as horses enter the stream at full speed driven by the Rzachdumba horse guards. Through that open door Aluk Shiang Cheung can see too a part of the many camps of men who await his pleasure. The men wander from campfire to campfire and from tent to tent. Without even being the One Who Knows he can be sure that in each group they talk about him and about little else, though guns are sometimes shown and cartridges exchanged. He sees three men trying out a rifle and a second later a sharp report follows the flash. Some of the Chinese soldiers leave their camp on the run to join the marksmen and then one turns back to return with his own gun. There is more shooting and others gather.

That is part of Chinese power: cartridges in unlimited quantity. With Chinese power one could do much, but Chinese interference is so hateful. The advantage of Chinese rifles and cartridges only in the hands of Tibetans might be enough. Certainly the Chinese have great supply, for the shooting goes on: Chinese gunfire on the meadow; poorly directed but continuous.

While the ones who have come to his door so pass the time all the tribes await his words. Some are openly ready to obey, others are uncertain, and still others are ready to deny with force each claim. The Labrang envoy is there because Labrang is traditionally the rival of Ngawa. The delegation of Ngura is there because Ngura is hostile to Gurdu. Ta-tzen, Ko-tze, Samtsa, Larengo— each name is stored in his memory since the old man first announced them—are all waiting to obey, perhaps, if it will further, too, the satisfying of their own feuds and grudges. What those other furtive hangers-on want is not so clear. And of Ah Ta he knows the least of all: Ah Ta the bold, who has been away somewhere for over a month. Back of all these promissory allies is the declared protection of the Chinese government if he should wish to profit by it. The camp of alien tents, so ill at ease, is best proof of that.

But who of all those men, representative of the peoples of Amdo, really believes in him—Aluk Shiang Cheung of the Precious Magic? Rather Aluk Shiang Cheung the Lama without—. But that no longer matters. His hat of special style will take care of that problem when he gives audience. Only to himself need he be the Earless One. Still he waits from day to day, uncertain when to begin. How long however, will those men camped along the stream be willing to wait? And how dare he keep the Chinese officer waiting?

"With reverence—with reverence—."

A shadow darkens the threshold and the doorway fills with shoulders almost too broad to enter.

"With reverence—Om mani padme hum!—My Lama—my Lama—."

The monk is on his knees inside the door.

"My Lama—the Earless One—."

The words are the terrible words no one else could ever dare say but the monk speaks like one saying his prayers.

"My Lama the Ear—."

The voice of the kneeling monk falters. As his eyes grow accustomed to the subdued light within, the face he sees under the special miter is not the face of the Earless One he carried on his back through the forest. Where are the two red scars that first claimed his startled pity and won his allegiance?

"Om mani padme hum! The lama knows! But you are the Earless One?" he pleads and the faith of a lifetime hangs on the answer.

"I am the Earless One."

The lama crushes his special hat behind him and turns his mutilated face so the monk can see and be satisfied. He now knows how and when to begin. He is ready for the envoy from Labrang; for the delegation from Ngura; for each and everyone of all who camp upon the plain. He is ready for Ah Ta himself, and when the Chinese officer comes he will be ready for him most of all.

"You shall be the one to pour my tea and carry this pistol. Only learn to draw it very fast or not at all. We shall go to Gurdu Great House together, for you are my 'resembling one' of the broad shoulders."

In the faith of one man who believes in him for himself, and has no grudge to satisfy nor ambition to further, he is sure of himself and of the future. To the one who carried him when helpless and saw him in the farce of his recapture he is uniquely the Earless One. So to all he will be the Earless One. To his one disciple he gives the first order.

"Go call all who want to see me. Tell them that Aluk Shiang Cheung is ready. Yes, ready even to see the Golok from whose tent I started on pilgrimage to Lhasa. Go tell them all to meet me in front of the yurt door. There the Earless One will speak words fit for their ears."

The monk goes on the errand and the door is left open so the lama may see the carrying out of his order. Soon he will meet all those whom he waited in vain to meet for three long years, and in addition to all the others, the representative of the Chinese government for whom he never waited and whom he never thought to see. He will make a great speech. Memories of another speech stir in his mind and he mutters to himself.

"The Earless Lama of Gurdu has come. Now at last I know what lama I am."

So he has come to the men gathered at the door of his yurt, and to all of Amdo who wait with words on their lips, the words which are like a creed of the future,

"The lama knows—with reverence—only the lama knows."

EPILOGUE

As earlier noted, the lama and I never met, but before, during, or after the events of the tale, he must have héard of me, for in 1960 I learned that "the Lama Without Ears" had arrived in India and was enquiring as to where I might be? He since has disappeared mysteriously into that border area along the great mountains, where Chinese troops and the soldiers of India warily watch each other across a shifting no-man's-land; and it is rumored that he has been assassinated. Others wonder whether he has not perhaps gone on to take the place he claimed in the Gurdu Great House. Either, or neither, could be the saga's ending but, again, only "the lama knows."

N4